NORTH
TORONTO

Traffic was not a problem in North Toronto in 1910.
This well-dressed gentleman is cruising south on Yonge Street. The picket fence and concrete
sidewalk mark the northeast corner of Broadway Avenue and Yonge.

A work crew of 14 men and 8 horses widen Yonge Street in preparation for the laying of streetcar tracks and pavement. This picture was taken in 1923 near Glengrove Avenue, looking north down the hill towards the entrance to Lawrence Park.

NORTH
TORONTO

DON RITCHIE

Stoddart

A BOSTON MILLS PRESS BOOK

Canadian Cataloguing in Publication Data

Ritchie, Don
North Toronto
Includes bibliographical references.
ISBN 1–55046–011–0

1. North Toronto (Toronto, Ont.) – History.
2. North Toronto (Toronto, Ont.) –
Pictorial works.
3. Toronto (Toronto, Ont.) – History.
4. Toronto (Toronto, Ont.) – Pictorial
works. I.Title.

FC3097.52R58 1992   971.3'541
C92-093913-9
F1059.5.T686R58 1992

© 1992 Don Ritchie
Design and Typography by Daniel Crack,
Kinetics Design & Illustration
Printed in Canada

First published in 1992 by
Stoddart Publishing Co. Limited
34 Lesmill Road
Toronto, Canada
M3B 2T6

A BOSTON MILLS PRESS BOOK
The Boston Mills Press
132 Main Street
Erin, Ontario
N0B 1T0

The publisher gratefully acknowledges
the support of the Canada Council, Ontario
Ministry of Culture and Communications,
Ontario Arts Council and Ontario
Publishing Centre in the development of
writing and publishing in Canada.

Looking north on Bayview Avenue from Eglinton in 1910. The house on the right was owned by Robert Cook,
of a North Toronto family that raised cattle and sold meat both wholesale and retail for over a century.
The inset shows what 80 years have done to Bayview Avenue.

CONTENTS

Yonge   and   Eglinton   in   1952

FOREWORD

NORTH TORONTO'S present is perhaps too strong for its past. There are people here who know more of the background of some quaint English village than of the background of the community in which they live. This book seeks to remedy that lack of awareness.

Henry James' duchess said: "We love history, don't we?...We like to know the cheerful, happy, *right* things!" Such an attitude may well apply to this book, an innocent thing, more story than formal history. We have simply fitted what facts we know about the North Toronto area into their appropriate time frames. There are nearly two centuries of actions and transactions, of births and deaths, but the humanity of it all, the happiness, perspiration and sorrow, must be imagined by the reader. Occasionally glimpses of real life come through; as, for example, in this resolution in the 1865 minutes of the York Township Council at Eglinton: "That the sum of $5.00 be placed in the hands of John Ross for the relief of Jane O'Hare, provided that she...will consent and allow her child to be bound to some reliable person." Or perhaps in designer-engineer Walter S. Brooks' quiet pleasure when he was allowed to lay out Lawrence Park in relation to the landscape rather than in the standard gridiron pattern. There is so much that we don't know. Perhaps this book will elicit new facts and unrecorded memories from informed readers — it is to be hoped in the form of new information rather than corrections!

Our story ends in 1954, the year that the subway reached Eglinton Avenue, a time when postwar changes in attitudes and lifestyles prevailed, to say nothing of the physical changes in North Toronto.

This book was written at the behest of the North Toronto Historical Society and has been underwritten by that organization. Three successive presidents, Alex Grenzebach, John Goodwin and John Hutchinson, were concerned and helpful. A book committee provided valuable assistance, particularly in modifying the rustic ebullience of the writer. Lynda Moon, the history specialist of the Northern District Library, provided the most welcome support of that organization, as well as her own sound knowledge of local history.

The book was started by, and should have been written by, Fiona Sampson, but her commitment to the concerns of Canada's native peoples has taken rightful priority over this project. Many people have been helpful. Alan Gordon, Julian Bernard, Elspeth Shtern, Bill Ramsay and Professor Wallace Judd spring to mind, but there were many others whose interest in the project made it a pleasant task.

DON RITCHIE   TORONTO 1992

An Introduction

People and Places

VERY EARLY ONE MORNING in August 1954, a row of policemen with loaded shotguns stood near the corner of **Mt. Pleasant Road** and **Lawrence Crescent**. Nearby, a number of citizens stood armed with a variety of weapons. The signal was given and a public address system broadcast a recording of the squallings of young starlings. The great Lawrence Park starling shoot soon exploded into violent action. No account of dead birds was kept, but the plague of starlings that had fouled the air, and the sidewalks, of the area was ended, for a time at least. That roll of gunfire in Lawrence Park was the most dramatic fusillade in North Toronto since the Rebellion of 1837.

Jon Vickers, the world-famous operatic tenor, sang in a North Toronto church while studying at the Royal Conservatory of Music. At that time Vickers was just learning to control his magnificent voice, and sometimes the quiet Presbyterians of **Glenview Church** wondered if he might actually lift the roof off the building.

"Willowbank," the home of the Gartshore family, became the clubhouse of the Toronto Hunt Club (Eglinton Branch) in the 1920s. In the 1930s it became a private home again. But in the 1960s it was bought and rebuilt into three spacious apartments by **Peter Demeter**, whose name has since become notorious. (Not only was Demeter convicted of having his wife murdered, but for a number of years he allegedly tried to arrange other murders from inside jail or while out on parole.) By 1990 "Willowbank" had regained its quiet dignity.

North Toronto has been, and still is, home to many distinguished lawyers, two of whom deserve special mention. **Roy Kellock** of **Sheldrake Boulevard** became a justice of Canada's Supreme Court, while **John R. Cartwright** of **Blythwood Road** became Chief Justice of that august body.

In the early years of this century, philosophical newspaperman **Alfred Smythe** lived at **22 Glengrove Avenue**. He is perhaps best remembered as father of the famous **"Conn" Smythe**, the World War I and II hero responsible for the building of Maple Leaf Gardens.

Lionel Pretoria Conacher was one of a family of ten children born to working-class parents down by the railway tracks south of St. Clair Avenue. His athletic ability soon became evident. In 1920, at the age of 18, in his first boxing competition, he became the Canadian light-heavyweight champion. The following year he fought a three-round exhibition bout with the great heavyweight Jack Dempsey. Conacher went on to become the obvious choice as Canadian Athlete of the Half-Century. He was big, powerful, fast and co-ordinated, remarkably good at lacrosse, baseball and football (his punting was incomparable). He was late in learning to skate, but within a few years was a star defenceman with the Chicago Black Hawks and later the Montreal Maroons.

Conacher's popularity gave him the chance to enter politics. In 1937 he became the Liberal MPP for Toronto Bracondale, and in 1949 the federal MP for the riding of Toronto Trinity. Known as "The Big Train," Conacher lived on Teddington Park Avenue and was a popular North Toronto citizen. He died of a heart attack in 1954 after hitting a triple in a charity baseball game.

This spot on Yonge Street south of Albertus Avenue marched on with the times. At the turn of the century it was a blacksmith's shop. In 1907 it was Mr. Ledder's livery stable. By 1920 it had become a garage offering repairs to Chevrolets. In the 1930s it was French & Head Motors. By the 1980s it was a clothing store.

By 1908, at the age of 21, **Charles Thomas Longboat** was the toast of world athletics. Tom Longboat was a splendid distance runner at a time when distance running was the queen of athletic events. He was an Onondaga Indian born on the Six Nations Reserve in 1887. He won the Boston Marathon (1907) and the "World's Professional Marathon Championship" (1909). In the controversial 1908 London Olympics marathon, both Longboat and Italian runner Dorando Pietri collapsed, probably from drug overdoses. Longboat continued to set records for many years, but sadly, by the 1930s he was working as a street-cleaner in North Toronto. Longboat served in two wars, latterly as a Veteran's Guard. He died in 1949 and was buried with full Indian ceremony. In the traditional way, his coffin was nicked to allow his spirit to join his ancestors.

Number **539 Blythwood Road**, fronted by low stone walls, was once the gatehouse and chauffeur's lodge of the Edgar Eaton estate. The road ran south down the hill to the main house still standing on Sunnydene Crescent. Today it can only be reached from Bayview Avenue. To the west of the big house was the gardener's "cottage" with a picturesque dovecot; it has since been converted into a most attractive home.

Not all the stone wall on Blythwood Road belonged to the Eaton estate. A section running west from Bayview Avenue is all that is left of the estate of **Frank Proctor,** a Toronto diamond merchant. The house itself was reached by a roadway which came out

at the exact corner of Blythwood and Bayview, and that wound slightly uphill through an orchard to a spacious one-storey home built of the same stone as the estate wall.

Magistrate **James Edmund Jones,** popularly known as "Judge Jones," had a house built at **181 Dawlish Avenue**, one of the first houses in Lawrence Park. Jones had been head boy at Upper Canada College and had won the Prince of Wales Scholarship to the University of Toronto. He became Deputy Police Magistrate of Toronto and developed an interest in helping underprivileged boys. He founded the Aura Lee Club for that purpose. The first clubhouse was at Avenue Road and Pears Avenue. Later an Aura Lee rink was built on the valley floor north of Blythwood and just east of Mt. Pleasant. A rough clubhouse was built nearby, but this burned down soon after being built. Jones and a magistrate friend from Montreal took teenage boys on canoe trips in Algonquin Park. One big canoe held eight paddlers and all their gear; it was made of tin and came apart for portaging. Jones was also an expert on hymnology, and wrote books on a number of religious and outdoors subjects.

Two very important but self-effacing public servants lived on **Glencairn Avenue** between Rosewell and Avenue Road. **Edward M. Ashworth** joined Toronto Hydro at its inception, and by 1924 he had become general manager. During his 42 years of service, he led Toronto Hydro through its growing pains and on to become a huge and efficient

These two pictures were taken from the same spot, but 70 years apart! Both look towards the corner of Merton and Cleveland streets. The left picture was taken in 1916. The house just visible to the right centre can be seen as the second house from the corner in the right picture, taken in 1986. What gentle changes hath time wrought!

The "PREVENTORIUM" garden, tended by happy childern in the care of the I.O.D.E. Children's Hospital, which was located on Sheldrake Boulevard from 1912 to the 1960s. The house at the left served as a residence for staff nurses. (Sometimes the nurses did not pull down their blinds, and one gentleman who enjoyed the view found himself spending several days in jail.)

public utility. **Tracy LeMay** served the City of Toronto for 44 years and was the city's planning commissioner for 25 of those years, a period during which the city experienced its most dramatic and critical growth. LeMay prepared the original extensive zoning by-laws. He was the first president of the continent-wide Institute of Professional Town Planners. Both Ashworth and LeMay died in 1954.

Alexandra Boulevard still has yellow brick gateposts at its Yonge Street entrance. In 1910 **J.H. Kilgore** (no relation to the Bayview Kilgours), just moving into the Toronto area, wrote to his son in England, telling him to ride his bicycle "about six miles or so up Yonge and then turn west at the yellow brick gates to your new home at 146 Alexandra Boulevard."

In the 1930s a quiet millionaire named **Gilbert Labine,** a governor of the University of Toronto, a member of the Order of the British Empire and one of the most influential men on Bay Street, lived at **63 Lympstone Avenue**. Though seemingly very much a member of the Establishment, Labine had a background which was more unusual than anything dreamed of by Horatio Alger. Born near Pembroke, Ontario, Labine left school early. By the age of 17 he was off to the rock country with his Winchester rifle, blankets and prospector's hammer. For 20 years he ranged the Canadian Shield with varying success, gradually moving north and west. In the spring of 1930, while prospecting near Great Bear Lake, his hammer broke into the most significant strike in the history of Canada. He had struck pitchblende containing uranium. At that time there was only one-half pound of uranium in the world: it was worth $2,500,000 an ounce. Labine's strike made possible the atomic bombs for Hiroshima and Nagasaki, as well as valuable medical advances. During World War II the Canadian government expropriated the Eldorado mine, but Labine, continuing as manager, built the huge processing plant at Port Hope, Ontario, and developed other mines. He died in 1977, in an apartment on Avenue Road. *The Globe and Mail* noted that "most of the pioneering sourdoughs who roamed...the Precambrian Shield...have become faceless characters of a half-forgotten era. The spectacular exception was Gilbert Labine."

Mount Hope Cemetery, at the east end of Erskine Avenue, was donated as a Roman Catholic cemetery in 1897 by private subscription, with Eugene O'Keefe as its organizer. It was opened in 1899, at which time a lot cost $14.97 plus $17.28 for perpetual care. The first burial was that of Edmund Sullivan, on March 27, 1900.

North Toronto has been home to many university faculty members, among them **Harold Innis,** for whom Innis College is named. Innis lived on **Chudleigh Avenue** in the 1920s and 30s. In 1937 he became head of the University of Toronto's political economy department. He was a pioneer in the field of communications. He had been a telegrapher in World War I. He was a quiet, unassuming neighbour whose stature as a scholar became evident only after his death. His wife, **Mary Quayle Innis**, was also a scholar of note. Her book on the economic history of Canada was the standard textbook on that subject for thousands of postwar students in Canadian universities.

E.J. Pratt was one of Canada's best-known and most distinguished poets. For many years he was a professor of English at Victoria College, where he influenced generations of students. He received many honours, and the Pratt Library at Victoria University was named after him. Pratt was a confirmed North Torontonian from the time that he arrived from his native Newfoundland. He lived in three successive houses, first 25 Tullis Drive, then 47 Glencairn Avenue, and finally 21 Cortleigh Boulevard. Pratt was a man equally at ease quietly writing poetry or drinking and talking far into the night with a group that called themselves "Canada First."

Mossie May Waddington grew up on Blythwood and Glengrove avenues. She had a brilliant university career and was a notable Greek scholar, as well as an excellent tennis player. She married and, as Mossie May Kirkwood, became Dean of St. Hilda's at Trinity College. Kirkwood Hall was named in her honour. It was a ritual for female Trinity undergraduates to be invited in small groups to Dean Kirkwood's for tea. The girls went with some trepidation, as the small Kirkwood children were being raised according to the system favoured by a notable Toronto psychologist, Dr. Blatz. Under this system, if a child kicked a visiting tea drinker, the visitor was obliged to kick the child back!

When the Pears brickyard was sold to the city as a site for **Eglinton Park,** much of the purchase price was put into the three-storey **Pears building** at **2409 Yonge Street**. Inside were 20 bowling alleys and 8 English billiard tables. Snooker was the most popular game on these tables, but some customers preferred English three-ball billiards or even Russian billiards, a very specialized game utilizing small wooden pegs.

Internationally famous editor and author **Thomas B. Costain** lived at **22 Lytton Boulevard.** He was at that time the editor of *Maclean's* magazine, but left in 1920 to become the senior associate editor of the famous *Saturday Evening Post*. Later he turned to writing and created 25 novels, histories and biographies, including *The Black Rose*, which sold two million copies. Another notable North Toronto writer was **Marshall Saunders**, who lived on **Strathgowan Avenue**. She wrote a touching book for young people, *Beautiful Joe*, which sold over a million copies.

One of the world's largest craters, located near Ungava Bay in northern Quebec, was discovered by and named after **Frank Chubb,** who was raised in a house at **184 Sherwood Avenue.**

Allan Lamport, one of Toronto's most outgoing mayors, grew up in his family's home at **182 Alexandra Boulevard.** He is remembered for lowering taxes and for introducing Sunday sports to this hitherto straight-laced city.

At the southwest corner of **Duplex** and **Glengrove** stands the house known as **"Leptis Magna."** Although one of the earliest homes on the street and one of the largest, with 27 rooms, it came to public attention only in the 1950s, when French engineer **Antoine Corege** bought it and began to lavish his artistic attention upon it. At first he won a homeowner award in a Beautiful Toronto campaign, and the house was put on the list of sightseeing tours. But as his adornments multiplied, the neighbours objected. The house, with its ornate additions, remains unchanged as of 1990.

A number of well-known artists have lived in North Toronto, including **Lawren Harris** and **Frederick Varley**. **Arthur Lismer** lived at 69 Bedford Park Avenue. (The current Lord Thompson Gallery displays a small Lismer painting entitled "Poppies on Bedford Park Avenue.") **Franz Johnston** lived at 135 St. Germain, **Herbert Palmer** at 170, and **Carl Schaefer** at 157 St. Clements. **Bertram Brooker,** an abstractionist, was at 107 Glenview. **Manley McDonald** lived on Highbourne Road, and many of his paintings were done in or near Garland's Bush at the east end of Lawrence Park. **A.J. Casson** lived in Lawrence Park.

Mill Pellatt, younger brother of Sir Henry Pellatt of Casa Loma, lived at **47 Glencairn Avenue.** (Their father, Henry Pellatt, was the first president of the Toronto Stock Exchange.) Mill Pellatt was head cashier of the Toronto and Niagara Power Company. Dressed in stiff collar and dark suit, he rode a bicycle to and from his downtown work-

Sir George Yonge was the Secretary for War in the British government and great friends with Governor John Graves Simcoe. When a road was cut through dense forest from York to Lake Simcoe in 1794, it was named Yonge Street in honour of their friendship.

place. When he moved to Stibbard Avenue, the house at 47 Glencairn was taken over by E.J. Pratt, the noted poet.

The Davisville Potteries operated in the community for 87 years (1845-1932). This lengthy period of activity, however, is challenged by the **Cooks of Davisville,** whose meat market closed in 1988. Although this retail butcher shop was opened only in 1929, the Cook family were in the North Toronto meat business as early as the 1850s, when three Cook brothers occupied three of the four corners at the present Davisville and Mt. Pleasant. For some 135 years the Cooks were in the business of raising and shipping cattle, butchering, and wholesaling or retailing meat in the Davisville area. At least two other butcher shops have provided over 50 years of local service. Both are still active in 1990: **Healeys,** who moved to Yonge Street from Dupont Street in 1925, and **Cowiesons** at Bedford Park. The oldest currently active business in North Toronto is **Milnes Fuel Oil Limited**. (Like the Davisville pottery, Milnes has changed its formal name once or twice.) Three generations of the Milnes family have operated the fuel-oil business from their location at Merton and Yonge.

St. James Bond United Church on Avenue Road has nothing to do with author Ian Fleming's super-spy character. It is simply the combined congregations of the Bond Street Congregational Church and the St. James Square Presbyterian Church.

Postal Station K, at the corner of Yonge and Montgomery, is unique in that it is one of the very few public buildings to carry the insignia of Edward VIII, the British king who "gave up the throne for love" in 1936 and infuriated many conservative, monarchist citizens. •

MERTON STREET looking west towards Mt. Pleasant Road on November 6, 1918. The Davisville Pottery is at the left where today stands a "Pottery Playground." At this time a private bus ran out Merton and thence to the Leaside flying station.

Q u a n d a t   I n d i a n

*T*HERE was an Indian village in the North Toronto area some 500 years ago. Dr. Mima Kapches of the Royal Ontario Museum has directed this artist's (Ivan Kocsis) rendition of the Quandat village. We are looking west from high above Eglinton Park. St. Clements Avenue would run from front to back at the right of the village. Roselawn Avenue would run through the left side. Avenue Road would run from left to right through the middle of the site. Modern-day Eglinton Park occupies the bottomlands in the foreground.

The Quandat lived in longhouses shared by approximately 40 people, all of whom participated in the construction and maintenance of the dwelling. The main crop was corn, as seen in open areas outside the palisade and on the valley floor. In the far right more space is being cleared by burning trees and stumps. Later European pioneers would have steel axes, but the Quandat had only stone tools.

There is an interesting continuity to this site. In 1837 John Montgomery built here, partly because of the springs that flowed out of the hillside. James Lesslie, a later owner, called his estate "The Willows" because he could grow those water-loving trees at almost the top of the hill. In the 1890s the Town of North Toronto pumped its water supply out of these very springs.

It is also noteworthy that the Indians needed a good supply of clay for pottery. From that same hillside came the clay that enabled the Pears brickyard to become a major supplier of bricks for North Toronto homes.

Village

THE BEGINNING

The signing of the TORONTO PURCHASE in August 1788. It was with considerable ceremony that Lord Dorchester met with the various chiefs and principal women of the Mississauga people.

FROM THE BEGINNING, Toronto was blessed with an excellent location. A main portage route reached Lake Ontario just where a spacious bay provided shelter. The water teemed with fish, the marshes with waterfowl. And just a few miles inland, high above the marshes, lay the delightful topography of what is now called North Toronto.

The earliest reliable evidence of human habitation in North Toronto dates back to about 1450. This date is based both on the oral tradition of the Indians and the findings of archaeologists. David Boyle, the first professional archaeologist in Ontario, reported that this area "abounds in traces of aboriginal manufacture." These settlers of over 500 years ago are thought to have been one of the four tribes known as the Quandat, which means islanders or dwellers on a peninsula. Whether the name applied to their geographic location or to their cosmological beliefs, we do not know. It was long afterwards that the French changed the Quandat name to "Huron," a derogatory Old French name meaning hairy or bristly knave.

The Quandat lived well, in a most favourable area of the country. The Quandat settlement in North Toronto is now formally known as the Jackes (Eglinton) Indian site. Franklin Jackes was the owner of the property when David Boyle undertook the first archaeological investigation there in 1887.

The Quandat believed that the individual was part of the universe, not the centre of it. General native cosmology maintained that every object had a soul. This was central to the Quandat's world view and determined how they interacted with their environment. They felt a responsibility for the welfare of the animal kingdom and for the ecological balance. Great emphasis was put upon respect for each person's dignity and independence. Corporal punishment for children was almost unheard of, and public opinion weighed heavily upon anyone who went beyond generally accepted limits. Women were respected as equals. Husbands worked side by side with their wives in the domestic fields. Moreover, we know that Iroquoian tribes traced their ancestry through their mothers rather than their fathers. Medicine men, and women, usually associated physical ailments with problems of the spirit. If the soul could be eased, then the body could take care of itself. This has a curiously modern sound! The Jackes Site was probably occupied for no more than 25 years. The Quandat had no knowledge of fertilizers or crop rotation. Once the soil was exhausted, they simply moved to a new site. The Royal Ontario Museum is presently investigating evidence that another site was situated just to the west of the Jackes Site.

The Quandat were a comparatively peaceful people, but they were not pacifists. Among the artifacts found on our site is pottery that was made in what is now upper New York State. This suggests that the Quandat probably sent raiding expeditions to that area.

By the mid-1600s raiding expeditions had turned into savage wars, leaving a large area south of Lake Simcoe as a no-man's land. Over a century later the British found the nearest permanent group of Indians to be a small group of Mississaugas living along the Credit River.

In August 1788 the little sailing vessel *Seneca* dropped anchor in Toronto Bay. Lord Dorchester himself, Governor-General of the Canadas, had come all the way from Quebec City to dignify the occasion. With considerable ceremony, the Mississauga Indians sold to the Crown a tract of land stretching from the present Scarborough, west to Etobicoke Creek, and running north from the lake some 28 miles.

The price was 1,700 pounds sterling, payable in cash and other things that the tribe wanted — kettles, blankets and carrots among others. It is difficult for us to evaluate this deal today, but there is no evidence of pressure on the part of the British government, and the Mississauga received what they asked for. It was land that the Mississauga used very little; their main settlement was on the Credit River.

A few years later, doubts arose as to the legal description of the grant. Did it really cover the land right up to Lake Simcoe? Peter Russell, the senior local administrator of the time, wrote in 1798: "Should the whole of that transaction be invalid, as your Excy. and Lord Dorchester have judged it to be, the King's right to any part of the land between the Rivers Etobicoak and Don, may become very doubtful." It was decided not to pursue this matter.

The little Town of York was established on the shores of Toronto Bay, but it faced the lake, mentally as well as physically. Few Indian moccasins or British boots trod the upland area between the Don and the Humber. The future site of North Toronto remained almost entirely a forest. "The pines were from one foot to six feet in diameter and the largest were five hundred years old and as tall as a seventeen story office building. Nothing grew at the base of these enormous trees. The forest shut out all the sunshine and most of the daylight.... A solemn roar, like a muffled waterfall, could be heard day and night," wrote Eric Hounsom in *Toronto in 1810.* •

THE JACKES SITE

December 20, 1887

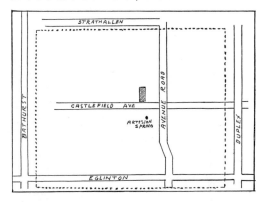

THE JACKES SITE *was located on present-day Castlefield Avenue just west of Avenue Road and was first reported by archaeologist David Boyle on December 20, 1887. The dotted outline in the map shows the location of the great palisade fence that enclosed the Quandat village. It has been estimated that as many as 30,000 persons lived here in 1645. Many splendid artifacts of Huron and Iroquois manufacture were found during excavation in a basement on the Franklin Jackes Estate.*

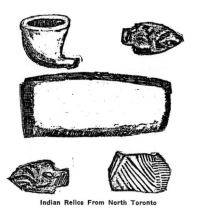

Indian Relics From North Toronto

NORTH TORONTO AND YONGE STREET

Part-time soldiers, most-of-the-time labourers, the QUEEN'S RANGERS started cutting Yonge Street through a dense forest of beech and pine trees up to six feet in diameter.

Instead of following the ancient — and relatively level — trail to Lake Simcoe, Colonel Simcoe opted to build a straight military road a few miles to the east.

N ORTH TORONTO really began in early spring 1794, at the spot where Yonge Street and Eglinton Avenue now come together. There, in that deep, solemn forest, some 30 men of the Queen's Rangers started to clear a road running north to Lake Simcoe. The road was to be called Yonge Street. The sound of axes, the clanking of chains, the curses and "gees" and "haws" as horses and oxen dragged the logs into piles for burning, all signalled the coming of European civilization. By the end of May the Rangers had reached the present Sheppard Avenue. Behind them lay a pathway through the forest. Not really a roadway, it simply dodged the larger stumps and forded the streams. Some of the ravines were too steep to be attacked directly. At York Mills the road took the gentler slopes well to the east; that route still exists and is called "Old Yonge Street." But the Rangers had provided a route — in some places almost a tunnel through the forest — that could be followed with assurance if not with comfort.

It was Lieutenant-Governor John Graves Simcoe's idea to extend Yonge Street off into the wilderness. He envisioned it as a shortcut to the Upper Great Lakes. It would be two years before Yonge Street was opened southward as far as Yorkville. For some years an informal trackway wandered off to the east and down to what is now Parliament Street. The extension of Yonge Street directly southward to York (called "the road to Yonge Street") was not completed for several years. Even as late as 1801 the road was "not passable for any carriage whatever on account of the logs which lie in the street." In 1797 Balser Munshaw, a German immigrant, took his Conestoga wagon apart to get it past parts of Yonge Street.

In Britain, where Simcoe was born and educated, thoroughfares were called roads. Only a few ancient Roman military roads were called streets. So it was with a sense of history that Simcoe called Yonge a street. George Yonge, for whom the street was named, was an old friend of Simcoe's and a member of the British Antiquarian Society, as well as Secretary of War. Yonge never visited Canada.

Even before Yonge Street was opened there was keen rivalry for the lots fronting it. To the right people, Upper Canada offered land that was both fertile and free. Simcoe planned to settle the area with United Empire Loyalists, or those who had fought for

Britain in the American War of Independence. No claim of multiculturalism can be made for the early settlers on this part of Yonge Street. They were either from the British Isles or from allied German states. The Ruggles, Bonds and Kendricks were originally English; McDougalls, McBrides, McGlashans and Mercers were Irish or Scottish in origin; the deHoens, Snyders and Pabsts were originally German. None of the area's early settlers had come directly from their homeland: all had spent at least ten years in America, giving them the necessary introduction to the rigours of settlement.

The first settler to be granted land in the area was Joseph Kendrick, and his property was 200 acres at the northwest corner of Yonge and what is now Lawrence Avenue. Other grants followed rapidly; most of the area was allocated by the early years of the nineteenth century.

There was no easy way to Yonge Street. Settlers had come hundreds, if not thousands, of miles of rough travelling to reach Upper Canada, and then they faced solid forest, heavy clay soils for the most part, and a winter even more severe than they were used to.

The overriding problem was the forest. Trees were the enemy, and for the first few years the pioneer spent most of his time clearing a few acres along his road front. The trees were felled, then cut into about 16-foot lengths or burned. Leaves and brush were piled up and burned. Logs were dragged into piles by oxen or horses. The homesteader was fortunate if he had his own yoke of oxen, like John McBride at the corner of Bathurst and Lawrence. If not, he could rent oxen by the day or week from Seneca Ketchum.

It was not enough to cut down the trees; there remained the stumps to be cleared out. It took from seven to nine years for maple or beech stumps to rot to the point where they could be removed. Pine stumps never seemed to rot: stump fences dating from pioneer times can still be seen in Southern Ontario, and they are always pine stumps. The Yonge Street settler planted potatoes, pumpkins, onions and even wheat by hand amid the stumps. Even as late as 1810, few of the lots had as many as ten acres properly cleared.

The second major problem was the climate. The settlers' first house was almost always a log house, about 16 by 20 feet, with an earth floor. Two small windows would be covered with oiled paper rather than glass. (Can you imagine window glass being bumped and banged up the St. Lawrence portages?) A stone or sometimes even a sticks-and-mud fireplace and chimney were used for cooking and heating. In winter the fire burned briskly, with a good upward draft; in summer smoke would suffuse the cabin and help to keep down the mosquitoes.

Clothing was improvised. European-style footwear was not practical for the Canadian winter, and the Indian style of moccasin was adopted. (In the 1920s North Toronto children commonly wore "shoe packs" in the winter, a sort of ankle-height moccasin worn over very heavy socks. One hundred years earlier Seneca Ketchum was selling "shoe-packs" at his store in Bedford Park.) Everything from carpeting to deerskin was put to use as winter clothing. Men often wore blankets, Indian style. Women wore the heaviest shawls they could find.

As the axe was to the pioneer man, the iron pots and pans were to the pioneer woman. Cooking was done over the open fireplace, with the pots hanging from hooks that could be raised or lowered as a rough means of temperature control.

A steady supply of food was a third problem — and there an open mind was absolutely essential. Mrs. Simcoe, the Lieutenant-Governor's wife and very much the English gentlewoman, served and ate some remarkable dishes. She mentions breakfasting off "a boiled black squirrel," and she served her guests tiny turtles on the half-shell. Raccoons were considered a delicacy, and there were always passenger pigeons that could be killed by the hundreds and salted down in barrels. Deer were plentiful in North Toronto, and there was a local market for the skins. Salmon were available from the Don River. Pigs were allowed to run wild, and were hunted and shot when needed.

Cows were the first choice in livestock, but they were costly. Seneca Ketchum sold one at 20 pounds sterling. Andrew Mercer and his family came up through Pennsylvania, crossed the Niagara River at Black Rock near Buffalo, thence to York Mills, with a cow tethered to the back of their Conestoga wagon. A law required good split-rail fences along Yonge Street, but cattle strayed in spite of that. James Ruggles advertised that he had found a stray calf, and that the owner could claim it for the price of the advertisement. Within a few years settlers had established distinguishing marks for their livestock: a cow with a hole in its left ear, a pig with no tail, etc.

Pioneer meals were "heavy, frugal, greasy and sustaining." Meat was not a very important part of the diet, although pork and any local wild animals were eagerly seized upon. The settlers' own produce — vegetables, eggs, maple or black walnut sugar, together with apples, pears and plums, and especially cornmeal mush — provided a well-balanced diet. But every item meant work: planting and pruning trees, feeding the hens, tapping trees for sap, hunting deer, and so on. The well-to-do, of course, ate remarkably well. In *The Town of York 1793-1815*, Edith Firth writes of James Ruggles and Joseph Willcocks, just the two of them, sitting down to a nourishing meal of "a salmon, two perch, a piece of roast beef, a brace of pheasants, rashers, and peas."

For most people it was a life of hard work, perhaps a good antidote for the homesickness and loneliness that many of the settlers must have felt. Social occasions were infrequent at first. The religious services held in Seneca Ketchum's home in 1799 may have been among the first. But help in building cabins for newcomers led to parties of a sort, with food and dancing. Yonge Street people came to know one another and to form a community of their own. Neighbourliness was a simple necessity in the rough life of settling in.

The original settlers were a mixed lot, and even included one man with a title. Baron Frederick deHoen was a nobleman and a former officer in one of the Hessian regiments that fought for Britain in the American War of Independence. He was an unlikely figure in the rather restricted society of little York, but he was popular as a 40-year-old bachelor. DeHoen received grants of land totalling 3,000 acres for his war services. Of these, 400 were in what is now North Toronto. On the northwest corner of Yonge and Eglinton he built the first two-storey building on Yonge Street, a log home that was to provide a haven for refugees in the War of 1812.

As a gentleman, deHoen was one of the seconds in the famous Smith-White duel in 1800. And in 1801 he was a second in another intended duel, one with an all-North Toronto cast. The main parties were to be "Lawyer" Weekes, who briefly owned Lot 3 (Sheldrake-Blythwood), and Joseph Willcocks (Forest Hill up to Eglinton). The seconds, oddly enough, were deHoen and his next door neighbour, James Ruggles. Somebody talked, with the result that Sheriff Jarvis arrested Willcocks in the dawn's early light, and the court forced the would-be duellists to keep the peace.

Just before the election of 1800 deHoen was sent up to woo the German settlers at German Mills (Leslie-Finch area) because he spoke their language. It was not a wise move. It was true that he spoke German, but the aristocratic gentleman in gloves was hardly the person to influence the tough, hard-working farmers who had come 450 mostly trackless miles through the Pennsylvania mountains in their Conestoga wagons. They listened to deHoen, and they took the bread and rum that he brought, but they voted against the government and elected Samuel Heron, a Yonge Street miller and distiller. DeHoen was a recognized leader in the settlement of the North Toronto area, but he gradually sold off his 3,000 acres. He is said to have given 400 acres for a horse that he especially favoured. His popularity seemed to diminish with poverty; he did not serve in the War of 1812, and he returned to Germany about 1817.

James Ruggles came to York with excellent credentials. Born to a prominent Massachusetts family, he was actually the sixth generation of Ruggles to be born in North America. His uncle, General Timothy Ruggles, was a notable Loyalist who raised

Council-Office, Dec. 29, 1798.

YONGE-STREET.

NOTICE is hereby given to all persons settled, or about to settle on *YONGE-STREET*, and whose *locations* have not yet been confirmed by order of the PRESIDENT in council, that before such locations can be confirmed it will be expected that the following CONDITIONS be complied with:

First, That within *twelve months* from the time they are permitted to occupy their respective lots, they do cause to be erected thereon a good and sufficient dwelling house, of at least 16 feet by 20 in the clear, and do occupy the same in *Person*, or by a substantial *Tenant*.

Second, THAT within the same period of time, they do clear and fence *five* acres, of their respective lots, in a substantial manner.

Third, THAT within the same period of time, they do open as much of the Yonge-Street road as lies between the front of their lots and the middle of said road, amounting to one acre or thereabouts.

JOHN SMALL, C. E. C.

a regiment to fight for Britain in the War of American Independence.

We don't know why James Ruggles came to Upper Canada; he had originally immigrated to New Brunswick. However, he was quickly recognized, made a magistrate and then a member of the four-man Executive Council of Upper Canada. He received land grants of 1,200 acres. Two hundred of these acres were on Yonge Street, immediately north of Baron deHoen's land. The grant covered the Roselawn to Briar Hill section and ran west to the survey line that is now Bathurst Street.

One of his early cases as magistrate concerned a young woman of considerable spirit. Esther Dunham was the daughter of a Loyalist, and she was charging another woman with assault. Her opponent claimed that Esther had started the fight. The case was adjourned while witnesses were found. Magistrate Ruggles had been able to study the plaintiff from the bench and he liked what he saw. When the case came up again, it was dismissed, as there was no Miss Dunham to press charges. She had become Mrs. Magistrate Ruggles on December 4, 1801.

Lye was made from wood ashes, and soap was made from boiling lye with accumulated fats and greasy bits. Macbeth's witches had an easier time than this.

C·W·JEFFERYS

The couple started right to work on a farm and a family. In three years they added three small boys to the population of Yonge Street. Esther's younger sister came to live with them. It seemed to be a happy story, but tragedy struck. As part of his duties, Ruggles had to try a case at Presqu'ile, near Brighton. The entire court, with witnesses, defendant and his entire tribe of Scugog Indians, set out aboard a little vessel called the *Speedy* on December 14, 1804. A tremendous storm came up, and the *Speedy* was lost with all hands. Widow Ruggles was left to carry on. Two years later her sister's dress caught fire, and in spite of Esther's efforts, the poor girl died of the resulting burns. But the Ruggles' farm remained a prominent feature on Yonge Street until 1836, when Esther sold it to the Hon. James H. Price. It became his estate of "Castlefield."

Joseph Kendrick was the first to receive a farm land grant in what is now North Toronto. The Kendrick family was from New England, having emigrated from Devonshire in the early 1700s. Most of the family were seafarers. Joseph's father, John, was formerly of His Majesty's 22nd Regiment of Foot. At the turn of the century, John Kendrick was Constable of York.

For a short time it appeared that John Kendrick's sons might take over much of the property north of Lawrence Avenue. Four brothers owned four consecutive lots on the west side of Yonge from Lawrence right up to Hogg's Hollow. But they were not farmers at heart. Duke William Kendrick did try; in 1799 he advertised that he was opening a "pot ash" on his lot, somewhere near the present Woburn Avenue.

North Toronto's first industry was not a lasting success. Within three years Duke William sold out and moved on to become an innkeeper and lake captain. His brother Hiram leased and then sold his lot to Seneca Ketchum. John Kendrick Jr. moved almost immediately to the London area.

Joseph kept his lot and alternated farming with being a ship's captain and owner. One early York report states that "Mr. St. George has just received by Capt. Kendrick, L.P., Madiera wine, Jamaica rum…and the best Spanish cigars." His first sailing vessel was named the *Peggy*, but by 1804 he had a larger ship called the *Governor Hunter*.

All four Kendrick brothers applied to be put on the official Loyalist list. They were informed that they needed have no such "pretensions," but somehow Duke William and his wife did make the list. One of the other brothers' wives, Sarah, received 200 acres by proving that she was a descendant of the famous Admiral Rodney. And the Kendrick brothers' mother, Dorcas by name, when widowed was recommended for 200 acres, but it was specified that the land must be "anywhere but on Yonge Street!"

The Reverend Thomas Raddish was an Anglican clergyman who was appointed Rector of York. His contact with York was very much a December-June affair: he arrived in December 1796, and he was gone by the next June, clutching the deeds to some 6,000 Upper Canadian acres in his ecclesiastical hands. He remained the absentee Rector of York for another year and a half. Finally, the pleas of his York parishioners induced him to write, from a very fashionable residence in London, to say that he would not be returning because "the pittance is too inconsiderable." He retained ownership of his 200 acres at the southeast corner of Eglinton and Yonge until 1816.

John Mills Jackson had the lot south of the present Mount Pleasant Cemetery (St. Clair to Glen Elm). He was a gentleman of 38 in 1800, born on the island of Barbados and educated at Oxford. A visit to Upper Canada impressed him greatly, and he bought several properties (he seems never to have lacked for money). He built a fine house (Heath and Yonge) which he called "Springfield." Jackson was an activist, and he wrote articles critical of the government. This earned him the name "Radical" Jackson, distinguishing him from "Hatter" Jackson, a Quaker on Yonge Street who made hats. Jackson returned to England for a few years, leaving his house untenanted and considered by local children to be haunted. When he did return, he moved to Lake Simcoe, where Jackson's Point recalls him.

Stillwell Willson had the 200 acres immediately north of the present Mt. Pleasant Cemetery. He was a son of the Loyalist John Willson, who operated the King's Mill on the Humber. Early in his career Stillwell was in charge of weights and measures on Yonge Street, ensuring that everyone used the same size of bushel and the same weight for a hundredweight. Stillwell was seldom still. He sold his first lot in 1804, and went on to buy a farm in the Finch-Yonge area, then to be an innkeeper in York, then part owner of two grist mills at Oriole, where he probably built the first part of the now-restored Henry farmhouse.

Thomas Hill and his family also had come the long way to this part of the world. Thomas had come to America from Somerset, fought with the Loyalist forces in the War of Independence, and had been exiled to Nova Scotia. In the mid-1790s he had come to York, joined the Queen's Rangers for a time, and then settled at the northwest corner of the present Sheppard and Yonge. In 1804 he bought and moved to Lot 5 West

In 1799 Duke William Kendrick advertised that he was opening a "pot ash" on his lot, somewhere near the present Woburn Avenue.

ASHES, ASHES, ASHES

The subscriber begs leave to inform the public that he is about to erect a POT-ASH upon Lot No. 7, West side of Yonge Street; where he will give a generous price for ASHES; — for house-ashes NINE-PENCE per bushel, for field ashes SIX-PENCE, delivered at his pot ash. He conceives it his duty to inform those who may have ashes to dispose of, that it will not be in his power to pay cash, but merchandise at cash price.

(Chatsworth to Lawrence). With the aid of his son, William, he cleared the land, although an old cabin was already there. The Hills opened a tavern in 1804, just one year before John McDougall's tavern at Glengrove. William proved to be a carpenter and builder, and much later, a grandson was a prominent Toronto contractor.

Hill and his heirs held parts of that property for nearly 75 years. The families' marriages show how close a community Yonge Street would become:

> *MARY and ANN HILL married ISAAC and WILLIAM HOLLINGSHEAD, brothers from the Thornhill area. The Hollingshead family were Loyalists from New Jersey.*
> *HARRIET HILL married RICHARD HERON, probably a relative of Andrew Heron, miller and distiller at "Big Creek" (The Don).*
> *HANNAH HILL married GEORGE BOND, whose father had been a captain in the King's South Carolina Regiment. The Bonds bought a farm in the Keewatin-Sherwood area in 1829, but they probably lived on Yonge Street in the old Thomas Hill house, just north of Chatsworth.*
> *WILLIAM HILL, the only son, married HANNAH MONTGOMERY, sister of the soon-to-be-famous John Montgomery. At that time the Montgomerys lived on Yonge in the area now known as Newtonbrook.*
> *Hannah's sister STATINA MONTGOMERY married STILLWELL WILLSON, and another sister, MARY ANN, married ANDREW MERCER, whose farm overlooked York Mills.*
> *Within one generation the cousins from these families formed a network up and down Yonge Street. A further involvement came when Mary Heron married John Snyder of a family with equally wide-ranging cousinships.*

The turn of the century saw Ruggles and deHoen as the most respected men in North Toronto, but with Ruggles' death and deHoen's slow descent into poverty, other settlers came into prominence.

Seneca Ketchum came to North Toronto from New Jersey via New York State. He first leased and then bought Lot 8 (Fairlawn to Deloraine). He was in some respects the most admirable of the settlers. He sold the north half of his lot to his brother for one pound, and then settled down to run a service agency and store for the district, combined with a small tannery and cobblery on the side.

Seneca kept an account book that recorded transactions in his store between 1806 and 1824. Everyone in the district is mentioned at one time or other, from "Old Finch" to "Captain Van Haen," "Major St. George" (Quetton St. George, prominent merchant in York), "Judge Sherwood," and "Wm. Jarvis Sheriff." They all bought their boots from Seneca, as did the Viscount de Chalus, one of the French aristocrats who escaped from the French Revolution and settled at Richmond Hill.

Seneca could rent you a yoke of oxen by the day or week, pasture your horse or cow, provide someone to chop your firewood, sell you a deer, or a pair of salmon from the Don, or 1,000 shingles. He would buy the woollen cloth woven by some of the farm

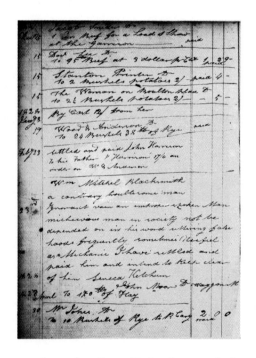

A page from Seneca Ketchum's account book.

wives during the winter. He was trusted throughout the district. If you wanted to trade apples for butchered hogs, Seneca's judgment was accepted.

The first school in the area was founded by Seneca Ketchum just behind the present Jolly Miller tavern. The first church services were held in his house, and he contributed heavily to the costs of building the first St. John's Church, York Mills. When he and his wife died, they left their Yonge Street property to King William IV, who was "graciously pleased to accept it" towards the building of the first, and much-needed, asylum in York. Up until that time, people with mental problems had been simply left in jail.

The more famous Jesse Ketchum was also an early citizen of our area. He came to York at the age of 17 on the *Speedy*, the same vessel that was later lost with James Ruggles aboard. Jesse lived with his brother until 1804. His biographer says that he then moved to his Glengowan property in Eglinton, but he could not have owned this lot until at least 20 years later. More probably, he moved down to the Davenport-Yonge area, where Jesse Ketchum School and Jesse Ketchum Park still exist and bear testimony to Jesse's presence in the area.

Nancy Love was a young widow with a year-old daughter, Lily. Her husband had been killed by a falling tree. Of necessity, Nancy became housekeeper for Seneca and Jesse Ketchum, both of whom were bachelors. It wasn't long before both men realized that Nancy would make a better wife than housekeeper. Seneca was 31 years old and Jesse was 25; Nancy was in-between, in more ways than one. The men solved the problem in a fine burst of brotherly love and male chauvinism: they drew lots for her. Jesse won the draw and married the widow Love. Although she had not been consulted, Nancy seemed pleased with the verdict. She proved to be an excellent wife and mother, contributing to Jesse's success. Little Lily Love remained a favourite with her stepfather, although the Ketchums soon had children of their own. Seneca did not grieve for very long. He soon married Anne Mercer, whose father's farmhouse looked down over Big Creek (as the Don was called) from the eastern heights near York Mills Road.

John McDougall was a highland Scot who had come to America in the 1750s. In the War of Independence, he joined the British side and worked in the Wagon Department of the army. After the war, like many Loyalists, he was transported to Shelburne, Nova Scotia, where he ran a store. Then he moved all the way to York, Upper Canada, where he opened a tavern. He tried to get land on Yonge Street as early as 1795, but it was not until 1803 that he moved to Lot 3 (Albertus to just past Alexandra). In 1805 his log cabin received a tavern licence. It would have been close to Alexandra and Yonge (fittingly, opposite the present liquor store).

When, as a Loyalist, McDougall's wife received 200 acres, they were in a position to buy the next-door lot (Glencairn to Glenview), and it was on this lot that grandson William McDougall spent his boyhood, making friends with the Indians who visited the Fox Creek Valley between the present Glenview and Chatsworth. William was later to become a Father of Confederation, and to lead a long and varied political career.

The McDougalls sold their earlier lot in 1811 to a Loyalist family named Snyder (sometimes spelled Snider). Along with his three brothers, Martin Snyder (b. 1748) had

HEY! THERE'S A FIGHT ON YONGE STREET!

Fights were not infrequent on our part of Yonge Street, and the fair sex carried its share of the fun.

1802   N. Jackson charged John Montgomery with assault.

1803   Jesse Ketchum charged Joseph Kendrick with assault. It was hard to get Joseph into court. He was a part-time lake captain; when his case came up, his brother John was there to point out that the wind was blowing from the wrong quarter and that Joseph could not get his vessel into port.

1804   Sarah and Mary Kendrick were found guilty of an assault on William Marsh.

1807   Stillwell Willson was found guilty of an assault on Patrick Caine. Stillwell had to post a bond of 40 pounds because he was not only guilty, but still very mad! One year later his victim came warily into town to remind the court that he still lived in "bodily terror" of Stillwell, who therefore had to leave his 40-pound bond for another year.

1808   John McDougall was convicted of assault and battery.

1809   Esther "Widow" Ruggles charged Henry and Catherine Hale with assault.

1810   Henry Mulholland was found guilty of assaulting Jacob Miller.

1810   Eleanor McBride was found guilty of assault on Jacob Cummer.

been sentenced to death in New Jersey for his Loyalist views. The Snyders escaped to New Brunswick, and after 20 years they took the long sea, river and lake voyage to Upper Canada. They settled on a site near Lake Ontario, until the mosquitoes drove them north to Lot 3 near Lytton Boulevard. The Snyders were a family that would expand to three farms within a few years and would influence North Toronto long after most of the earlier settlers were gone. They will be heard from later.

Jonathan Hale was 21 years old when he reached York at the turn of the century. At a time when people were on average almost six inches shorter than today, he must have cut a fine figure — six feet tall, fair-haired and blue-eyed. He was a tough, direct and energetic man, the prototype of the Yankee individualist. He was one of the few settlers in the area who was not brought into court for fighting; probably no one wanted to challenge him. During the War of 1812 Hale publicly "damned the King and Constitution" and got away with it.

In 1803 he married Margaret Carey and bought her father's farm. A few years of hard work saw Hale in possession of a splendid farm of 400 acres — Lawrence Park, from Lawrence Avenue south to almost Blythwood, and of course from Yonge to Bayview. His household consisted of 11 people, including 5 young children. His house was close to Yonge, at the top of the hill at Glengrove East. When Jesse Ketchum bought the Glengrove property, he built a new house further back from Yonge Street, but Hale's house and outbuildings were part of the estate and were still standing almost 100 years later.

For years Hale proved himself to be "a man of much usefulness in his day in the promotion of public works." In the late 1820s he sold his Lawrence Park farm to his son-in-law, his Glengrove property to his three sons, and then he quietly disappeared from the Yonge Street scene.

We can visualize Yonge Street in 1810, threading its narrow way past stretches of forest interspersed with clearings. It was becoming a well-used route, but still a bad road. In 1807 a Toronto paper reported that "a lot of people last Saturday turned out to cut down the steepness of the Yonge Street hill" at what is now filled-in land holding the Rosedale subway station.

For our purposes, we can start just north of St. Clair Avenue. This immediate area had been called "the poplar plains" from the earliest times, and so we can assume that it had been burned over and was just filling up with the earliest trees (poplar, birch, etc.). The overwhelming feature from about Heath Street north was the forest, through which the road provided only a narrow slit. In some places the trees would meet overhead, and even as late as 1810 there were still a few stumps that the track avoided. Men found guilty of various misdemeanors were often sentenced to remove one stump from Yonge Street.

Travellers of the day would go, not up Yonge Street, but up what is now Lawton Boulevard, in order to avoid an especially nasty ravine. To the east, just where Yorkminster Park Church now stands, the handsome house of John Mills Jackson stood in a bit of parkland. North of that was the property of Alexander Legge, who was notable for selling liquor to the Indians, and for marrying Grace Cawthra. His farm is now Mt. Pleasant Cemetery. This is the only original, unsubdivided 200-acre lot in the area today.

It is also the best way for a city person to visualize what 200 acres represented — remember that it ran, not just to Mt. Pleasant, but right through to Bayview.

We cross Mud Creek (Mt. Pleasant Creek) just west of Yonge and rejoin Yonge at about the present Davisville. There was a clearing here on the east side, the only one on either side all the way up to Eglinton. Some work has been done on the swamp at Manor Road, and they have laid down a corduroy road that "would undulate under the weight of a passing load"; the slippery logs were very dangerous to horses.

Eglinton Avenue, we think, was little more than a blazed trail to the west. To the east it was a track; some people came up the Don Valley to Eglinton and then across to Yonge Street. DeHoen's cabin was on the northwest corner of Yonge Street. There were clearings and the beginnings of farms on both corners on the east side.

From Eglinton north there were signs of real farms taking shape. Especially on the west side there were fields and fences, and the forest was being pushed back acre by hard-won acre. On the east side, there was a five-acre clearing at Sheldrake, and another at Lawrence where the Locke Library now stands. The whole west side of Yonge from Eglinton to Lawrence was a succession of serious settlers — deHoen, Ruggles, McDougall and Hill.

Lawrence Avenue was another trail, passable enough to let the McBrides and the Mulhollands through to their farms at Bathurst Street. Cleared land continued on both sides up to about Fairlawn, where Seneca Ketchum's store and rent-all was on the west side. Across from him, Lots 8 and 9 to the city limits and beyond remained Crown land until 1817. At the top of the hill the road, now Donwoods Drive, turned east and wound down to where Samuel Heron dammed the Don for his grist mill and distillery.

The keynote of the years before 1812 was simply unremitting hard work. Up the length of Yonge Street, the most common sound was the "chunk" of the axe. If you had money, like John Mills Jackson, or if you had great land grants to trade, like deHoen, you could pay to have your property cleared. But most of the Yonge Street families did it themselves. The rough log cabins amid fields filled with stumps gradually gave way to a few acres of recognizable farmland. •

TWO EARLY VIEWS OF SETTLEMENT LIFE

Stark. Bleak. No trees, only stumps. Cowpats. Horse dung. Pig manure. Smoke-blackened rooms. Unwashed, illiterate people…
                                    JANE LANGTON

When lamps and candles were hard to obtain, and the evening light was supplied by the blaze of pine knots…the little ones shared the rugs of bear and wolf skin with the favoured hound and shaggy retriever, while glancing light fell on the swiftly-plied knitting needles of the mother and old sister, and the father sat quietly enjoying rest from a day of manly toil.
                                    CATHERINE PARR TRAILL

THE
ORIGINAL
LAND
GRANTS

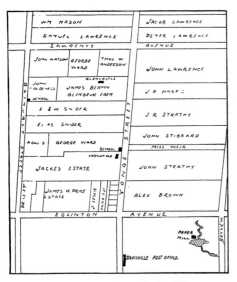

A Map of North Toronto in the 1870's

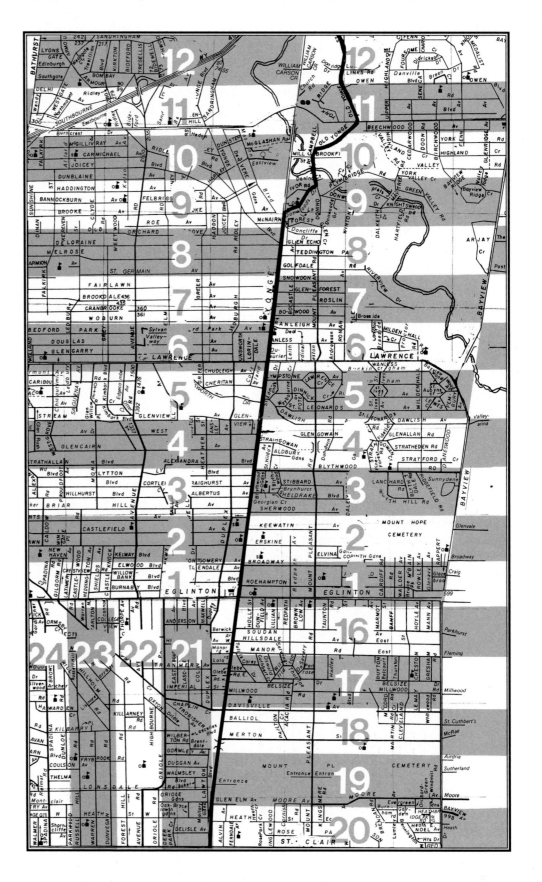

THIS MAP shows the original land grants in relation to a recent North Toronto map. The dates below are from the Registry Office and may vary by a few years from the dates on which the grants were authorized by committee: for example, both Joseph and Duke William Kendrick were in possession of their lots some years before the date shown.

ORIGINAL LAND GRANTS AND SOME SUBSEQUENT OWNERS

WEST SIDE OF YONGE STREET	EAST SIDE OF YONGE STREET

LOT		LOT	
1.	*1815?* Baron de Hoen, (see page 23)	1.	*1792* Albert Fessenden
	– 1833 John Montgomery		*– 1826* Jacob Snyder
2.	*1798* James Ruggles, (see page 24)	2.	*1798* Reuben Clark
	1835 James Price		1826 George Bond,
3.	*1803* John McDougall, (see page 27)	3.	*1803* Richard Gamble
	– 1811 Martin Snyder, (see page 28)		*– 1835* Jesse Ketchum, (see page 40)
4.	*1801* Jonathan Bell	4.	*1806* William Weeks
	1811 John McDougall		*– 1811* Jonathan Hale, (see page 28)
5.	*1801* Nathaniel Hewson	5.	*1797* William Cooper
	– 1804 Thomas Hill		*– 1808* Jonathan Hale
6.	*1800?* Joseph Kendrick, (see page 24)		*– 1836* Samuel Huson
	– Thence divided	6.	*1798* Bernard Carey
7.	*1800?* Duke William Kendrick, (see page 24)		*– 1829* Peter Lawrence
	– 1806 Jacob Herschmer	7.	*1817* Daniel Dehart
8.	*1804* Hiram Kendrick		*– 1834* Joseph Easton
	– 1806 Seneca Ketchum, (see page 26)	8.	*1817* William Marsh
9.	*1798* John Kendrick		*– 1820* Daniel Brooke Jr.
	– Thence divided	9.	*1798* Sammuel Heron
10.	*1806* Andrew McGlashan		*– 1821* Daniel Brooke
	– Thence divided	10.	*1796* Andrew Mercer
21.	*1815?* Baron de Hoen		*– Thence divided*
	– Thence divided	16.	*1796* Thomas Raddish, (see page 25)
22.	*?* Hon. Peter Russell		*– 1833* Charles Moore, (see page 52)
		17.	Clergy Reserves
			– 1836 Rectory of St. James
		18.	*1802* Stillwell Willson, (see page 25)
			– 1808 D'Arcy Boulton and Micheal Dye
		19.	*1803* Mary Ann White
			– Thence Mount Pleasant Cemetery
		20.	*1798* D. Smith
			– 1806 John Mills Jackson, (see page 25)

THE WAR OF 1812

T**HE WAR OF 1812** was not popular along the American-Canadian frontier: it had its origins far from Upper Canada. Britain was in a life-and-death struggle with the Napoleon's France. The British assumed the right to search American ships for British deserters, and the Americans were outraged. Loud American support for the war came from the southern states, where the "war hawks" voted solidly for war. In New York State and New England, on the other hand, the voting was two to one against war.

An American on the frontier wrote that "the news of the war was unwelcome on both sides of the (Niagara) river," and a Canadian reported that "both sides were in consternation: the women and children were out on the banks of the river, while their fathers, husbands, sons, etc., were busily employed in arming."

General Isaac Brock, who was sent to Upper Canada but who longed to be in Europe, where the action was, saved Upper Canada at the outset of the war. He achieved three brilliant victories: River Raisin, Detroit, and Queenston Heights. He died a hero on a Niagara hillside, unaware that his knighthood was in the mail. Two hundred of the York Volunteers, many of them from Yonge Street, fought at Detroit and at Queenston Heights.

Yonge Street settlers seem to have had mixed feelings about the war. Although the area had its share of old Loyalists, there was also an increasing number of Americans who had come to Upper Canada for personal betterment rather than political choice.

Several residents left for the United States. John Kendrick went to fight for the Americans. Widow Ruggles' brother, Charles, was captured in an American uniform and executed. Joseph Willcocks, after vacillating for some time, was killed while fighting for the Americans. Others left for less warlike reasons. "Hatter" Jackson was a Quaker who returned to the States but removed himself from any taint of war. He returned to Canada after the war and was accepted without rancour. Jacob Van Zant, a prominent tanner in York, sold his business and returned to the States. Jesse Ketchum was prompt and wise enough to buy up Van Zant's tannery and its soon-to-be-valuable property.

Familiar names also fought on the British side. Henry Mulholland fought in the battles of York, Lundy's Lane, and Stoney Creek. Thomas Humberstone, whose pottery was near York Mills, helped to carry the body of General Brock to the grave. Duke William Kendrick, who was christened Duke William, died in active service with the 3rd Regiment of York Militia. His brother Joseph served with the navy and was wounded. His small ship, the *Governor Hunter*, was commandeered and later sunk. Jacob Snyder fought in the army for a time and later provided horses for the army. It is said that he obtained a lot of these horses by simply taking them while their Quaker owners were at church!

Later Snyder received a veteran's pension and the respect of the community, who called him "Captain Snyder," although there is no evidence that he ever reached this rank.

The War of 1812 brought prosperity, or at least relative prosperity, to Yonge Street. The first effect was increased traffic. Hitherto, most of the heavy goods going north had gone up the Don River, or by trackway that ran beside it, and only came out on Yonge Street at York Mills. But by 1812 the lower part of Yonge Street had been much improved. The Northwest Company may have used Yonge Street to get supplies to its main staging base at Fort William. Heavy freight could be loaded onto wagons at the foot of Yonge Street. Below St. Clair, an ingenious winch helped to get heavy loads up the big hill.

Yonge Street proved its value in the early stages of the War of 1812. At one point a relief expedition of 250 officers and men was sent to reinforce the British-held U.S. fort on Michilimackinac Island. By using Yonge Street and the short route via Lake Simcoe, the force reached the fort in time and kept it, and the Upper Great Lakes, in British hands. In 1814 the captured crews of the U.S. ships *Tigress* and *Scorpion* were marched down Yonge, no doubt to the delight of local boys and girls. From time to time British Marines marched up Yonge Street in dramatic uniforms and packs. These troops were joined by somewhat less formal bands of sailors and straggling groups of shipwrights, artisans, cooks and labourers. Moving more slowly came wagonloads of supplies — foodstuffs, cannon balls, and all the paraphernalia needed to mount and maintain a war. Supplies were needed for the big naval base of Penetanguishene, as well as the fort on

THE BATTLE OF QUEENSTON HEIGHTS, October 13, 1813. Men from Yonge Street fought with the York Volunteers at the taking of Detroit and also at Queenston Heights.

33

Michilimackinac Island. Closer to hand, Lake Simcoe was on a war footing, for it was part of the main route to the Upper Lakes. Near Barrie, many bateaux were built, and there was a blockhouse at the site of the portage. As late as 1819 an armed schooner patrolled Lake Simcoe.

Down Yonge Street came an increasing stream of wagons loaded with food and supplies for the little town of York. It was a prosperous time. Taverns were needed to slake the thirst of travellers on the alternately dusty or muddy road. Presumably, John McDougall's tavern was still active (at Glengrove); certainly William Hill's was kept busy (at Lawrence). The widow Vallier's tavern at Big Creek (York Mills) was one of the most popular stopping places, since it gave drivers and horses a chance to pause before tackling the big hill. (Actually, going up *or* down was a difficult matter for a team of horses. Sometimes huge tree branches were tied on behind to act as a brake while going downhill.)

The price of foodstuffs rocketed, to the delight of local people. They felt they were suddenly being repaid for all the labour spent in clearing their land. Now their crops provided the means of buying more livestock and household and farm necessities. Prices finally reached the point where the government had to step in. Ceilings were put on the prices of wheat and most other foodstuffs, but it was a comfortably high ceiling. The only problem was that all distilleries were closed for a time in order to conserve grain.

The fighting came closest to the Yonge Street area in April 1813. Three local men with familiar surnames — John Montgomery, his brother-in-law William Hill, and Emre Lawrence — were returning some supply boats from Kingston to York. As they skirted the shore just off Port Hope, they saw a fleet of 14 American warships heading toward York. They promptly beached their boats and set off on the quick march to York, anxious to warn or to help. Neither their warning nor their help was of much use. The

Here, wearing top hats, are veterans of the War of 1812 photographed 50 years later at a garden party in Rosedale. Jacob Snyder of Eglinton, who fought with Brock and alongside Tecumseh's Indians, is fourth from the left.

1,700 U.S. troops that landed just west of York were too strong a force for the small troop of British soldiers, some local militia, and 60 Indians, some 700 all told, who tried to defend the town.

As the Americans began their attack, one York family decided to send their women, children, and one old man up Yonge Street to safety. They set off for the Baron deHoen's two-storey log home at Eglinton and Yonge. As chronicled in Henry Scadding's *Toronto of Old*, "Miss Russell stacked her phaeton so high with clothing and supplies that there was no room for anybody to ride in the carriage. The party straggled along behind it as it creaked and swayed over the corduroy roads." The ten unfortunate walkers included the aged Robert Baldwin, together with four small boys, one of whom had to be carried most of the way. Mary Warren Baldwin, a true romantic, had at first written that "nothing could equal the beauty of the [American] fleet coming in." This poetic viewpoint was shattered when the Fort York magazine, filled with 500 barrels of gunpowder, blew up with a tremendous blast. Rocks and debris filled the air. American General Zebulon Pike and many others were killed. Witnesses described the cloud of smoke that arose as being in the shape of a mushroom. The small Russell group, struggling up Yonge Street, "heard a frightful concussion, and all sat down on logs and stumps, terribly frightened."

Not far from deHoen's cabin, quite possibly in one of the local taverns, there was a mixed reaction to the landing of the American forces. James Finch (of Finch Avenue) "rejoiced at the coming of the American fleet." Jacob Lawrence (of Lawrence Avenue) "favoured the enemy with his gestures and conversation." Jonathan Hale "damned the King and Constitution for taking public property" (perhaps Jacob Snyder had crossed Yonge Street and taken some of Hale's horses). These quotations are taken from the *Register of Persons connected with High Treason* that was kept during the war. Someone was listening and reporting, but nothing seems to have been done as a result of these disloyal statements.

The Americans did not stay long at York. Before going, they burned the small frame Parliament Buildings. An unconfirmed story is that the British, in retaliation, attacked and burned the presidential mansion in Washington. Whitewash was used to cover the charred parts of the building, and resulted in the name White House.

By 1814 Napoleon was banished to Elba, and Britain turned its attention to America. Seasoned troops could now be spared for Upper Canada and the Royal Navy could now blockade American ports. Peace followed almost immediately.

Yonge Street was still busy. One particular load must have provided a buzz of local conversation. A tremendous cast-iron anchor, large enough to require 12 oxen to pull the sled on which it rested, inched its way north, heading for Penetanguishene. There is uncertainty as to whether it came up the Don Valley or up Yonge Street. Certainly it was moved in winter, when snow and ice could help its progress. So heavy and tedious a task was it, that when peace was declared, the anchor was left right where it was. There it still sits, on the roadside just north of Holland Landing. •

POST-WAR GROWTH IN NORTH TORONTO

IN 1815, with the war over, Upper Canada settled down to being an out-of-the-way British colony administered by an unimportant British Lieutenant-Governor. It had none of the romance of India, none of the wealth of the West Indian plantations.

Local excitement prevailed briefly in 1815, when no fewer than eight local citizens were jurors at a rather strange trial. Two men named Cooper and Bannerman were charged with stealing "eight pieces of cannon and one howitzer" from the house of Lord Selkirk. Such a theft creates a vivid mental picture. It was a full-scale trial, with Attorney-General Robinson and Solicitor-General Boulton for the Crown, Samuel and Livius Sherwood, and W.W. Baldwin for the defence. The local jurors were George Bond, Jos. Sheppard, Peter Lawrence, John McDougall, Wm. Moore, Alex Montgomery, Jonathan Hale and John Willson. The accused men were acquitted. The law required that one could be a juryman only once a year, but this requirement proved impossible in early years and jury service became something of a regular occurrence.

Despite the usefulness of Yonge Street during the war, it was still nothing more than a dirt road. After rain, and in the spring, the mud made it virtually impassable. In 1815 there was no sign of a village that we could call the nucleus of a future North Toronto. Yonge Street ran through settlers' clearings that were slowly becoming farms. There were a few small taverns to provide food and shelter for tired travellers or those caught by nightfall. Roads were not necessarily safe at night.

The descriptions of Yonge Street that we have from that time suggest that much depended on the view of the beholder. In 1819 a visitor named John Goldie wrote, "This is the best road I have seen in Upper Canada.... There have been more wagons travelling this road than all those I have seen since leaving Montreal." These views were not shared by Lady Bond Head, wife of the Lieutenant-Governor (1835-38). She wrote, "There are dreary roads extending many miles with new cleared grounds and black charred stumps of trees and occasional huts and horses and farm yards which they call Yonge *Street*." Her husband echoed her views: "You drive into the everlasting forest."

He was wrong: it wasn't an everlasting forest. Trees were coming down every waking hour. Simcoe's *street* was proving to be a success. Not only had it proved its worth during

the war, but now it served as an artery into the Home District, as the area around York was now called. Settlers were taking up land, not only on Yonge Street, but east and west in little rural communities like Newmarket and Lloydtown. Closer to York, lots were being taken up on the concession lines both east and west of Yonge. Roads, more accurately trails, reached out to these areas. The most important crossroad in our area was what is now Lawrence Avenue. It extended west at least as far as "the Second" (Bathurst), where the Mulhollands and McBrides had settled. It went east even further, out to the Milne grist mill on Wilket Creek, now Edward's Gardens. Advertisements for this mill appeared in York newspapers, pointing out that it could be reached either by Mr. Hale's road (Lawrence Avenue) or by Mr. Mercer's road (York Mills Road). Use of the latter route very likely meant that "the Second" (Bayview) must have been passable at least down to Lawrence.

Improvements were still needed on Yonge. In 1819 a new bridge was built just south of the present Chatsworth Avenue. The Minutes of the Town Meeting in York reported: "Joseph Sheppard and Jesse Ketchum chosen a commity to Superintend the Building of a Bridge over the river between John McDougall's and George Bond's on Yonge Street." The bridge was called "Hawke's bridge," after the builder. Hawke went on to straighten

CASTLEFIELD (ca. 1856) *was built by James Hervey Price in the 1830s. The house stood on the south side of the present Castlefield Avenue. It is captured here in one of the earliest photographs ever taken in the Toronto area. It was a showplace of the district, an example of the romantic style called Gothic Revival, a deliberate return to the fancied Middle Ages. Sir Walter Scott would have approved of the battlements and Gothic windows. But if one looks closely, the house is not as big as its turrets suggest, and it may be a reornamentation of the old Ruggles farmhouse. The Jackes, who bought the property in 1844, are posed here with their household maids, standing shyly at the left.*

out Yonge Street at York Mills. A causeway was built to carry Yonge across the valley floor, and an enormous amount of grading and filling was needed on the ascent at the north end. What would be simple today was a major undertaking when a small scoop-shovel drawn by a horse was the only earth-moving equipment. It is worth noting that the scoop-shovel was used to excavate the basements for almost all the homes in North Toronto. Tractors and small backhoes were introduced in the 1940s and came into use in the 1950s. Of course, large steam shovels were used for major undertakings from the 1880s on, but not for a simple residential basement.

Split-rail fences and small barns were built to provide shelter for livestock. Stumps were pulled by draft animals with the help of men with axes; stump-pulling machines came only in the 1850s. Oxen were of tremendous importance during the years of heavy clearances. Seneca Ketchum rented out oxen. A pair could be bought for about 16 pounds. (Catherine Parr Traill, a serious observer and recorder of the time, noted that most teams of oxen in Upper Canada were named "Buck" and "Bright").

Horses became more common and more useful as clearing enlarged farms. By 1836 a good farm horse cost about $75. There were three main types of horses in Upper Canada at the time: "Conestogas" brought up from Pennsylvania by settlers; "French-Canadians" that infiltrated into the eastern districts; and Indian ponies that ran semi-wild around the Mohawk settlement on the Grand River. The Yonge Street horse probably combined the Conestoga and the Indian pony, with remarkable results which one visitor describes thus, in Edwin Guillet's *The Pioneer Farmer and Backwoodsman*: "This gallant little set of animals…were very merry goers. It was their wonderful sure-footedness, sagacity and docility however which delighted me. They were driven without blinkers or bearing reins, and where…bridges seemed doubtful, miry fords suspicious of quag-mires…they would put down their heads to examine, try the difficulty with their feet, and when satisfied, would get through or over places which seemed utterly impractical."

Year by year the forest was being pushed back and small log barns were built to provide shelter for livestock. Instead of being a problem, wood could now be sold in York. Orchards were beginning to bear fruit. The Baron deHoen sold 148 bushels of apples to Jesse Ketchum on one occasion (deHoen's orchard then stood right where Orchard View Boulevard now stands).

There was the beginning of industrial activity on Yonge Street, south of the present Davisville Avenue. Michael Whitmore operated a sawmill and a pottery on the west side of Yonge. He had dammed Mud Creek (later Mt. Pleasant Creek) for his mill, and the milldam served as the crossing for all who walked up or down Yonge. Historian Henry Scadding says that the end of the sawmill was open so that the actual sawing could be watched by the passers-by. At this early date the saws were long, straight, reciprocating blades driven up and down by water power. A ratchet device moved the log forward as the saw cut on the downstroke. (The circular saw was introduced in the 1840s.)

Scadding describes the pottery thus: "After crossing the dam of Whitmore's Mill, and returning into the more direct line of the street, some rude pottery works met the eye. Here in the midst of woods, the passer-by usually saw on one side of the road a one-

TO POTTERS.

GOOD encouragement given by the subscriber, three miles north of York, U. C. on Yonge-Street, for two or three Journeymen POTTERS that understand making Brown Earthenware.

MICHAEL WHITMORE.

February 23, 1826.   35tf

MICHAEL WHITMORE ran this advertisement in February 1826, seeking journeymen potters to make brown earthenware.

horse clay-grinding machine laboriously in action, and on the other, displayed in the open air on boards supported by wooden pins driven into the great logs composing the wall of the low windowless building, numerous articles of coarse brown ware, partially glazed, pans, crocks, jars, jugs, demijohns, and so forth, all which primitive products of the plastic art were ever pleasant to contemplate."

For 150 years the Davisville area was to remain the nearest thing to an industrial centre in North Toronto. By the 1920s Merton Street was an active business area, particularly the area still bracketed at Yonge by Milnes Coal and at Mt. Pleasant Road by the concrete silos of Dominion Coal and Wood. On the west side of Yonge, Rogers Coal, Sercombe the Mover, and other companies occupied the north end of Lawton Boulevard.

There had been very little real estate activity during the war. Children of the original settlers were now growing up. The period after the war witnessed many marriages, most of them involving near neighbours: Leonard Ashley and Sarah McDougall; Alex Montgomery and Rebecca Smith; John McDougall and Mary Porter; James MacMillan and

EARLY ONTARIO POTTERS

Yonge Street Pottery Burnt.—This valuable and highly useful establishment, the property of Mr. Michael Whitmore, an enterprising and patriotic inhabitant, has been burnt to ashes. It took fire on Saturday last, suddenly, and resisted every attempt to extinguish the flames. The loss of $1500 will fall heavy on the proprietor, but it is said that his neighbours, journeymen and friends intend to give him every aid in their power towards its entire re-establishment.

Millie Hale; Joseph Rushman and Clarissa Hale; Stillwell Willson and Statina Montgomery; Davis McBride and Amanda Hale; Joseph Huson and Nelly Cake; John Snyder and Mary Heron.

The Church of England was the only officially recognized denomination, but the government could license other ministers to perform marriages. Presbyterian, Baptist and Roman Catholic clergy had little problem in securing such licences, but Methodists were regarded with suspicion, as it was felt that they harboured dangerous American views. It was a time when democracy was a bad word. Major Graham, who settled at Bathurst and Eglinton, complained that all the schoolteachers in the area came from the United States.

People of the time also differed strongly from most people today in their views of capital punishment. In 1828 there was to be a hanging in York, and the schools were closed so that even the youngest could witness "the wages of sin." Ten thousand people, four times the population of the town, are said to have crowded around the jail to watch the hanging.

Major changes in the Yonge Street area began in the late 1820s. Suddenly there was prosperity and something of a real estate boom. When William Snyder married Nancy Cummer in 1827, he realized that he needed a home in keeping with the prosperity of the area in which he lived. He built just such a home for his bride, and it still stands, somewhat changed but clearly recognizable, on the west side of Duplex Avenue, between Lytton and Alexandra. It was built as a one-storey Regency-style cottage and probably

In October of 1830 Michael Whitmore's pottery burned to ashes. It appears that Whitmore continued to operate the sawmill, but that the pottery business was taken over by John Walmsley of Deer Park.

had a balcony running around it. It was a forerunner of a series of houses built in an area in which style was as important as comfort.

Some of the new homes were quite lavish, often surrounded by lawns and impressive driveways. Jesse Ketchum, a man of considerable wealth by this time, built a spacious home at the end of a driveway that became Strathgowan Avenue. The Hon. James Price bought the widow Ruggles' farm and built "Castlefield," the model of an English country estate. John Montgomery built a large and handsome inn at Broadway and Yonge, but then decided to retire, so he built a home on his farm overlooking Yonge and Eglinton. Samuel Ames Huson left his wealthy estates in Barbados and established an estate called "Kingsland," which crowned the peak of the present Lawrence Park.

About 1830 Jesse Ketchum moved back into the area. He bought 200 acres of the old Jonathan Hale farm. The old farmhouse was at the northeast corner of what is now Glengrove and Yonge. It was reported in 1836 that Lieut. Gov. Francis Bond Head was interested in buying this attractive property, but Ketchum would most certainly not have sold it, especially to Bond Head, who was a bitter personal enemy. In any case, Ketchum ignored the old Hale farmhouse and built a handsome new home where Strathgowan and St. Hilda's now meet. It was reached by a long drive bordered, within living memory, by orchards on either side.

Jesse Ketchum, (1782–1876) was a successful industrialist and financier. He named Temperance Street in downtown Toronto.

Jesse Ketchum was a self-made man. Despite the fact that he had never been to school, and despite an unhappy and at times brutal childhood, he had the gift of making money. The tannery that he had bought cheaply in 1812 had prospered. He had large real estate holdings in Toronto, Yorkville and Deer Park, as well as his new estate at Eglinton. In the meantime he made up for his lack of schooling: the local teacher lived at the Ketchums' and helped his host in the evenings. Although Ketchum had a pew in St. James Anglican Church in downtown Toronto, he made land available on his estate for a Methodist Church, yet he was happy to have one of his daughters marry a Presbyterian minister. He was prominent in the early temperance movement, founding the *Temperance Record* in 1836. In donating downtown property to the city, Ketchum specified that no liquor was to be served on his Temperance Street. This, of course, has since been ignored.

Ketchum's personal life had its ups and downs. In 1804 he married Nancy Love, a 26-year-old widow with a young child, Lily. The Ketchums raised five children: Lily, Fidelia, Mary, Anna Rose and William, sometimes called "Sonny" or "Young Billy." Lily and Mary married and moved away; Fidelia married James Harris, a young Presbyterian minister; Anna Rose died of cholera at the age of 21(her mother died six weeks later); two years later Jesse married Mary Ann Rubergal, a sister of Mrs. Price of nearby "Castlefield."

James Hervey Price was the first city clerk of Toronto, and the minutes of the inaugural meeting of the City of Toronto are in his handwriting. The Prices had come to Canada in 1828 and stayed for a short time in Dundas, Ontario, before moving to York. James studied law there and was called to the bar in 1833. In 1835 he bought the Ruggles' farm on Yonge Street for 1,000 pounds. It ran from the present Roselawn to past Briar Hill, and from Yonge to Bathurst.

On this property, and probably using the Ruggles' farmhouse as a base, he raised a house in the very latest style, a small neo-Gothic castle. Turrets and lancet windows made it distinctive. All interior woodwork was of black walnut, a fashionable wood at the time. The servants rubbed it down with buttermilk on a regular basis. A 24-piece set of sterling silver flatware and a corresponding set of fine china, all with the Price family crest, were custom-made in England. There were separate cottages for the farmer and coachman. Two streams ran through the property, which rose at the back to the highest spot within miles.

The Price and Ketchum farms were quite close together, and the two men shared a common sympathy with the political Reformers, though neither supported armed rebellion. It was therefore to be expected that they would become friends, despite their widely different backgrounds. It was not really unexpected that the recently widowed Jesse Ketchum should be attracted to Mrs. Price's sister, Mary Ann, and that the two should marry. The Ketchums and the Prices represented the high-society life of the 1830s.

For ladies such as the Price and Ketchum sisters, there was always much to do, even though they had servants to take care of the housework. Clothing, for example, took time. There were no ready-made clothes in Upper Canada; clothing for the family and servants were all made by hand. Shopping for cloth could be enjoyable. In 1826 an advertisement pointed out the choice in fabrics: "Broadcloths (all colours and quantities), cassimeres, satinettes, flannels; pelisse-cloths, baizes, fearnaughts, tartan and caroline braids; bombazettes, bombazeens, velvets; beaverteens, fustians, Circassians, vestings; steam-loom shirtings; a genteel assortment of calicoes, French and Indian silks, cambriels; imitation merino, silk, and cotton shawls; mull, jaconet, leno and book muslins, dimities, ginghams...."

Men like Price and Ketchum, who were regularly involved in financial affairs, were required to deal in a very complicated money situation: "In Upper Canada there was a value called 'currency' reckoned in pounds, shillings and pence...but this did not represent English pounds, but Halifax *or* New York pounds [all three differed from one another]...there was no coinage at all...What coins there were British pounds, United States dollars, and old Spanish dollars that were often cut up into bits. Two of these bits made up a quarter dollar. Many of the coins were defaced and had to be weighed to determine their value. Merchants issued paper, much in the way Canadian Tire stores do today...The Bank of Upper Canada later issued copper tokens for pennies and halfpennies. Besides this array, there were in circulation notes of hand and IOU's issued by the well-to-do."

Is it any wonder that barter was a common custom? Seneca Ketchum, in his store on Yonge, sometimes kept his accounts in pounds and sometimes in dollars!

In 1829 Seneca Ketchum left his store in order to fulfil a long-standing ambition. You will recall that Seneca had opened his house for the earliest church services, in 1799, and that later he had become something of a lay preacher. His ambition took him north and west into a wilderness that is now Dufferin and Grey counties. There he and his wife, Anne, visited every bush settler and over a period of years established nearly 20

JAMES HERVEY PRICE who converted the Ruggles' farm into "Castlefield," an estate fit for an English gentleman. Price was one of the gentry who supported the Reformers – but not to the extent of armed rebellion.

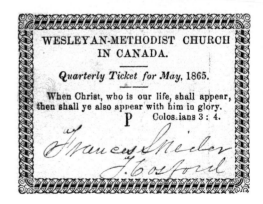

The Methodists who built this church at Yonge and Glengrove East in 1832 were not very popular with the officials in York. They were suspected of favouring democracy!

JOHN MONTGOMERY, who consigned his judge and his accusers to "hell's flames."

small missions or churches which he visited regularly. He died in 1850, far from his Connecticut home and worn out in the service of his Lord.

Not everyone had the strong faith of Seneca Ketchum, and it is more than possible that some went to church primarily to meet and talk to people. Nevertheless, there was a tendency to cling to their own denomination, the faith of their fathers. Seneca's wife, Anne (Mercer), tended to push him in the direction of Presbyterian, though he himself favoured the Anglican Church. There is some doubt therefore as to what we should call the first services held in the valley of the Don at York Mills. We know that in 1815 John Strachan preached in an old "school" with rain dripping through the roof. Jesse Ketchum's biographer, E.J. Hathaway, points out that "there was always a Presbyterian chapel there." It was 1816 when the first known church was built overlooking the Don Valley on the site of the present St. John's, York Mills. There is some evidence that the people who donated the land and built that first chapel intended it to be interdenominational. If so, they reckoned without the aggressive Anglicanism of John Strachan. It is said that the man who donated the land for the church was denied burial because he was a "non-conformist." Whether there was another chapel at York Mills remains doubtful, although services were being held in 1831 by Rev. Rintoul, a travelling Presbyterian.

At any rate, there were no churches in the immediate area of North Toronto. The first church there was built in 1832 on land made available by Jesse Ketchum close to his new home. The Hydro station at Glengrove and Yonge now stands on the site of this church, which stood for nearly 100 years. The deed conveyed the land to Peter Lawrence, Daniel McDougall, George Bond, William Snyder, Sheldon Ward, and William and Thomas Hill. The church was one of seven Methodist chapels on what was known as the Yonge Street "circuit," and it was called "the brick church" since all the other chapels were of frame construction. At a later date a fire blackened the brickwork, and the building was stuccoed.

John Montgomery was a man respected in the Yonge Street community. His father, Alex Montgomery, was a Loyalist who came to York from Stamford, Connecticut, via New Brunswick. It is said that the Montgomerys stayed with the John Beverley Robinsons upon their arrival at York. If so, they must have had impeccable Loyalist credentials, since the Robinsons were the *crème de la crème* of Loyalists. After serving in the War of 1812 the Montgomery family moved up Yonge Street to the place now called Newtonbrook, but which was soon called Montgomeryville. By 1830 John Montgomery was part owner of a tavern called The Bird in Hand that stood just north of Finch Avenue. He sold his half share of the tavern, but there are persistent reports that the frame building was literally sawn in half when he and his partner agreed to separate. Montgomery wanted a better future for his family, and therefore he bought the Baron deHoen's excellent farm at Yonge and Eglinton. In 1832, on the highest point of this farm on Yonge Street, he built a commodious inn that history remembers as "Montgomery's Tavern."

Montgomery was one of a family of ten children. During the course of a long life, he had three wives (scarcely mentioned in the reports of the time) and was survived by seven children. Just as the new inn was being completed, the Montgomerys had the sad misfortune of losing two daughters within ten days. It was the same year in which the Ketchums also lost two children in the same short space of time. Cholera was all too common in Upper Canada at the time. It was dreaded by all, because there seemed to be no defence or cure.

Traffic continued to increase on Yonge Street during the 1820s. The authorities began to lay gravel on some of the muddier stretches. In 1825 the local citizenry all came out to stare as Sir John Franklin led his second Arctic expedition up the road. In 1832 they watched a steam engine being hauled up Yonge Street on its way to Lake Simcoe, there to be installed in a steamboat called the *Peter Robinson*. It was the first sign of the Industrial Revolution in the area. (The first steam engine to be used nearby was at York Mills in 1848, where it powered a grist mill.)

George Playter of Newmarket started a "some-time" coach service down Yonge Street in 1828. Four years later it was absorbed by William Weller's coach lines. These coaches and sleighs, painted brilliant yellow, ran east and west from York to Kingston and Dundas, as well as north to Holland Landing.

At about the same time, two partners named Murray and Newbigging established a thrice-weekly freight service up Yonge. In the face of this kind of traffic, the authorities began to experiment with road improvements. They "macadamized" the road by tamping down several sizes of crushed stones so that they formed a very solid and well-drained roadbed. To help to pay for this, a tollgate was opened at Yorkville in 1820, and by 1830 another at the southern top of York Mills hill. The toll for a one-horse pleasure vehicle was twopence.

By 1835 the road was macadamized as far north as Eglinton, and in that year the Reverend Newton Bosworth wrote: "The traffic on Yonge Street is amazingly great, and almost resembles that of some of the roads leading to London, England...the said street...a great public road and has shorter intervals between the houses all along it than any road of the same length I ever saw in England...the 'clearings' extend a considerable distance on both sides of the road, and the former arboreous appearance of 'the bush' itself, is broken at intervals by numerous settlements."

Anna Jameson, looking back on 1837, recalled her drive through the Home District, and through "some of the finest land and most prosperous estates in Upper Canada. It was a perpetual succession...of well-cultivated farms. Some of the farmers are reputed rich men...yet all this part of the country was, within a few weeks, the scene of ill advised rebellion, of tumult, and murder." •

CONCOCTION FOR CHOLERA

In desperation, people grasped at concoctions like the following:

2 tablespoons	Ground Maple Charcoal
2 tablespoons	Hog's Lard
2 tablespoons	Maple Sugar

To be taken 2 tablespoons every half hour.

The SNYDER farmhouse, now 744 Duplex Avenue, was originally built in 1828 and is the oldest surviving building in North Toronto. It once stood at the end of an orchard-bordered drive from Yonge Street and remains as a patriarch among the somewhat newer homes on Lytton and Alexandra – a reminder of a time when there were only wheat fields and farms along Yonge Street.

THE UPPER CANADA REBELLION OF 1837

COLONIAL ADVOCATE.

Thursday, Nov. 22. 1832.

HUZZA FOR MACKENZIE !!!

To the Poll ! To the Poll !!

Gentlemen—*We expect to see you next Monday at the Election! Herein fail not!! Huzza for the County of York!!! Wake up! and awaken your sleepy neighbours!! Your rights are invaded!!! To the Poll!! To the Poll!!!*

Yonge Street, November 17th, 1832.
AT a Public Meeting held this day at Mr. John Montgomery's Inn, Yonge Street,

Political fevers were especially fierce in November 1832, so much so that the printer nearly ran out of exclamation marks as election time approached. To The Poll!! It is clear that the publisher favoured the Mackenzie faction!

YONGE STREET reaches something of a high point at Broadway Avenue north of Eglinton. You can see south to St. Clair and north to Finch Avenue. It is this modest high point that has gained a place in Canadian history as the site of the rebel headquarters for the "battle" of Montgomery's Tavern. The actual battle was fought in the fields to the south.

The Rebellion of 1837, in considerable measure, was brought on by William Lyon Mackenzie. The fiery little Scotsman fanned a smoulder of discontent into the blaze of rebellion. There were grievances, of course. For example, one-seventh of all land was reserved for the Church of England, yet Anglicans never did form a majority in Upper Canada. As the settler, or his horse, picked a careful way over the swampy road in the present Manor and Glebe area, it was a constant reminder that this ill-maintained road ran through one of the Clergy Reserves. There was discontent about the educational system and the high salaries of York officials. But most of all, there was resentment over the Family Compact, a small minority who controlled the government by working together as a clique. They were able to do this by having control of the appointed Executive Council, which could overrule the elected Assembly.

The Upper Canada Rebellion of 1837 was a very small example of a general movement towards breaking free of traditional shackles. The Spanish Empire in South and Central America had been broken into republics. In Britain, the Reform Bill of 1832 gave the vote to a section of the middle class, and in 1833 slavery was abolished throughout the Empire. In the United States, democracy was the new word. President Jackson is said to have sat with his boots on his desk and with his door open to all. In Upper Canada during the 1820s and '30s, there was continual friction between the Loyalists and the Reformers. Elections were marked by fights and small riots. The Family Compact, almost always with the support of the Governor appointed from England, remained firmly in charge. When Sir Francis Bond Head was sent from England, the situation deteriorated rapidly. Bond Head was a bad choice as Governor; he was as quick-tempered and as vituperative as Mackenzie. People were almost forced to take sides.

Much of the strength of the Reformers lay with the farmers north on Yonge Street, but the Rebellion of 1837 was not just an agrarian revolt; there were a number of prominent supporters of the reform movement. On Yonge Street, Jesse Ketchum and the Hon. James Price favoured reform. But when Mackenzie, in frustration, began to talk of armed rebellion, many of these moderate Reformers withdrew their support. Among the first to withdraw were those who had much to lose — Ketchum, Cawthra, and Doel the brewer could not run the risk of losing their considerable possessions. Doctors like Morrison and Rolfe held out a little longer, as theirs were not material risks. The Rebellion was led by radicals, but the troops were mostly young men who had little to lose property-wise.

In the autumn of 1837 men were drilling in the Don Valley west of Yonge Street. Bullets were being cast just north of Sheppard Avenue. December 7 was chosen as the

This C.W. JEFFREYS drawing captures the mood and costumes of the rebels marching down Yonge Street in 1837. The artist lived on the east side of Yonge just north of York Mills Road.

C.W. JEFFERYS

date for getting together to move on Toronto, and Montgomery's Tavern was chosen as the meeting place. The tavern was a handsome building. "Around the front of the house, which faced towards Toronto, ran a platform or stoop raised on three steps to avoid the slush in the spring thaws...On one side of the door was the usual large barroom, over the entrance a lamp, and before the house, a huge signboard raised on high, bearing the usual hospitable announcement." It was no simple roadside tavern. According to the *York Pioneer*, 1888, it was "100 feet by 70 feet, partly two and partly three stories in height. There were 27 rooms on the ground floor and 19 apartments on the second floor." Altogether there was accommodation for 100 people and stabling for 84 horses. Montgomery advertised that there was "a fair view of Lake Ontario on one side, and the Oak Ridges on the other."

John Montgomery was a prominent member of the Yonge Street community and a Reformer with reservations as to the use of armed force. He had decided to farm instead of keeping bar, and a new house had been built for him on the hill overlooking the present Eglinton Park from the west. By December 1837 the furniture was being moved into the new house, and his family was preparing to move in. John Linfoot had arranged to lease and operate the tavern.

Into the handsome hostelry, and into the midst of the moving of the Montgomery family, came the Rebellion. There was news from Toronto that the city was undefended and that an early attack was bound to be successful. This news failed to reach Mackenzie, who was out somewhere among the farms, but it reached Samuel Lount at Holland Landing. Lount, one of Mackenzie's chief lieutenants, "took the message as an order to jump the deadline and march south on Monday." Accordingly, small groups of men, bearing rifles, staves or pitchforks, started moving down Yonge Street towards Montgomery's Tavern.

After a hard day's work on the farm, the rebels gathered for drilling in the Don Valley just east of the present-day Bayview and Sheppard.

When the news did reach Mackenzie, he tried to go back to the original date of Thursday, but it was now too late. The rebels were already assembling.

By Sunday night 150 men had reached the tavern, and they were hungry as well as tired. Monday, Tuesday and Wednesday were days of uncertainty and confusion, both for the rebels at Montgomery's and for the Loyalists in the city. As more rebels arrived, food became a serious problem. On Tuesday groups were sent out to forage. The local farms were visited. Some gave quite willingly; others found that supplies were simply commandeered. They took meat from Nightingale's slaughterhouse (Bedford Park, west side), and later, when they took cattle from the Ketchum farm, they drove the beasts up to Nightingale so that he could slaughter them. They found quantities of oats at the neighbouring farms. (No doubt there were enough Scotsmen to make them into porridge.)

Later in the day a large group of rebels set off down the road to Toronto. Those who had rifles led the way, followed by those who had only pikes or pitchforks. Meanwhile, Sheriff Jarvis and a group of Loyalists were posted at Bloor Street. When the rebels reached Bloor, there was a short, sharp fusillade. The rebels retreated rapidly north on Yonge; the Loyalists retreated south. Left behind was one unfortunate man who had been killed by a more or less random bullet.

Wednesday found both sides regrouping. In Toronto, by this time Loyalists were gathering from east and west. A 13-year-old girl brought in the first news of the actual strength and condition of the rebels. Cornelia De Grassi lived with her parents on a farm on Don Mills Road. She had her own horse and often rode freely through the Don Valley area. Her exploit, which is mentioned in several documents of the time, is best told in the words of her father, Captain Philip De Grassi. He was a soldier, originally from the Austrian Empire, and he had taught languages in England. A man of considerable means, he had chartered a ship to bring his family across the ocean. He had settled east of the Don, and with dignity and composure, he watched his wealth slip away. At one point he lost his house for debts, and with wry humour he would point out that his youngest child was born in a manger. The present De Grassi Street is named after him. Captain De Grassi: "One of my daughters about 13 years of age...rode out under pretence of wishing to know the price of a sleigh, went to a wheelwright's shop close to Montgomery's tavern, and being suspected, was taken prisoner and order to dismount. To this, she demurred and during the altercation with her captors, Mackenzie came with the news that the Western Mail was taken...Amid the

DEATH OF COL. MOODIE.

general excitement, my little girl had the presence of mind to urge her horse to ride off at full speed amid discharges of musketry. A ball went through her saddle and another through her riding habit. Arrived in Toronto, she was taken before Sir F. B. Head, the Governor, to whom she gave valuable information as to the numbers and conditions of the rebels...and so my poor girl was the means of saving Toronto...." De Grassi may have exaggerated the outcome, but there seems to be no doubt that the girl actually carried out this remarkable feat.

By Thursday, December 7, the Loyalists were ready to move, and they did so in an organized and stately manner. As William Kilbourn tells it in his book *The Firebrand:* "At the head rode Colonels Fitzgibbon and MacNab; in the midst, Sir Francis, stiff and tiny, a hero again for the day, and black-coated John Strachan with a young priest attendant. Two cannon rolled north under the watchful eye of Major Carfrae, an artillery officer utterly content in his call from retirement. As the militia disappeared through the distant Bloor toll-gate, the sun glinted on bayonet and musket, and made sudden yellow flares of the brass, whose music carried away out of the city's sound and across the fields on a rising breeze."

The Rebels set up a blockade in front of Montgomery's Tavern to prevent news of the rebellion from reaching the city. COLONEL ROBERT MOODIE, a Loyalist, was shot as he tried to ride past the crowd. The tavern was located on the corner of present-day Montgomery Avenue and Yonge Street.

At Montgomery's Tavern, despite rumours of enemy action, most of the rebels were simply enjoying the noonday sun that was melting the snow on the frozen ground. A sentinel posted down Yonge thought he heard music. As he came up to report it, the sloped muskets could be seen coming up the hill at St. Clair, and suddenly the enemy was plain and menacing.

About 150 rebels with rifles were posted behind "snake" fences somewhere about today's Hillsdale Avenue West and Duplex. A few were posted on the east side. Most of the unarmed rebels with their pikes and pitchforks remained near the tavern.

It was the moment of truth. The Loyalists and rebels were face to face: Sir Francis Bond Head, with both his horse and his heart dancing with excitement; Bishop Strachan, looking as if he were the accredited representative of God, as well as the British Empire; on the rebel side, Mackenzie, wearing several overcoats as armour, foaming with excitement; and Samuel Lount, the Quaker, calmly determined to do what he could, but very much aware that he was in an impossible position.

Nearly 1,000 Loyalists faced perhaps 300-400 rebels, most of them without firearms. The first shot sent a cannon ball through the Paul Pry Tavern (at Glebe and Yonge). A volley of musketry sent the rebels flying from behind their fences. The next cannon shot went right through Montgomery's Tavern and sent the remaining rebels scattering into the fields and woods. It was hardly a battle at all (only one man was killed).

After that, all was anticlimax. Bond Head sent soldiers to see that no harm came to Mrs. Montgomery and the children, then he had Montgomery's Tavern burned to the ground. He described it as follows: "Volume after volume of deep black smoke rolling and rising from the windows of Montgomery's Tavern. This great and lofty building, entirely constructed of lumber and planks, was soon a mass of flames whose long red tongues darted horizontally, as if revengefully to consume those who had created them, and then flared high above the roof. As we sat on our horses the heat was intense."

Mackenzie escaped. There is a romantic story to the effect that he fled to "Castlefield," and that a large Irish cook hid the small Mackenzie in an empty cradle in the kitchen. It would be nice if it were true. More likely, he ran behind "Castlefield" and the Snyder and Murray farms before getting a horse at Lawrence Avenue and making his escape westward. Eventually, he crossed the American border.

David Gibson, in charge of the prisoners being held at the tavern, had set off up Yonge Street with his prisoners as soon as the Loyalist army appeared. Just south of Lawrence, he turned them east up the hill that is now Lawrence Park. He took them to the edge of the woods behind Mr. Huson's splendid new house, then, seeing the soldiers coming up Yonge, he left the prisoners free to go as they pleased. Gibson's own house (in Willowdale) was burned to the ground by the Loyalist soldiers. In the meantime John Montgomery, knowing that his family was safe, went across the road to William Snider's farmhouse, which was located somewhere about Sherwood Avenue. He was captured three days later.

There was a wholesale roundup of rebels and suspected rebels. Jesse Ketchum's son, William, was arrested, along with many other well-known locals — John McDougall,

John Anderson, William Kendrick, Robert "Stibbert," Joseph Sheppard, John Gibson, William Hill, Edward Snider, William Heron.

On the Thursday following the "battle," the people on Yonge Street saw a line of almost 500 men being marched to Toronto, "including one hundred and fifty Indians with painted faces and savage looks…Each prisoner…was tied with a rope." John Doel saw them as they entered the city "in midwinter like so many slaves driven to market…some of them were old grey-headed men — some without overcoats…some never saw their homes again, but perished through privation or neglect." Most were released after a few days, but for some, like John Montgomery, the story was far from over. He was jailed, charged with treason, tried and sentenced to hang. His statement to the judge at sentencing is a classic of its kind: "I consider that I did not get a fair and impartial trial. There are men here who have sworn my life away. The perjured evidence of W.B. Crew, Thorn, and Greenwood will haunt them in after years. They will never die a natural death and when you, sir, and this jury, and all who have taken part in my sentence and death, shall have died and perished in hell's flames, John Montgomery will yet live, and be residing on Yonge Street."

John Montgomery did come back to live on Yonge Street. One of his accusers shot himself; another cut his throat. Almost all of the people involved in the trial did die before Montgomery, but it has not been determined whether or not they perished in hell's flames.

Montgomery's sentence was commuted to transportation to Tasmania, but he escaped from the fort at Kingston. Despite a broken leg, he was able, with the aid of John Anderson, another Yonge Street rebel, to escape to the United States. Montgomery returned to Canada in 1849; Anderson stayed in the United States and became an honorary colonel in Florida, with a good deal of property there and in Wisconsin.

Nearly 40 years later Anderson came back to what was now Ontario, "to grasp the hand of his old compatriot. Colonel Anderson is about ten years younger than his old friend, and is hale and hearty as a man of fifty. The meeting between these two old companions in arms was as affecting as might be expected between men so identified with each other in the history of their country, and day after day was spent in reviving, amid tears, the incidents of their arrest, trial, sentence to death, imprisonment, escape, flight, and final pardon. On Thursday morning parting took place, probably the last on this earth between these two, and Colonel John Anderson started for his southern home."

Quite a number of people — estimated as high as 25,000 — left Upper Canada during or after the Rebellion. Most went to the United States, where there was still cheap land in Illinois or Iowa. Some later returned, but many others, like Thomas Alva Edison's grandfather, stayed on. •

PROSPERITY BECKONS IN CANADA WEST

JOHN THOMPSON'S coaches offered indoor or outdoor seating for the trip to Toronto. Service was provided from as far away as Holland Landing, but there were more frequent trips from Thornhill. This picture was obviously taken at a time when photographs were still a novelty.

ANIMOSITIES were not forgotten following the Rebellion, but the land was fair and prosperity beckoned. Upper Canada was abolished with the stroke of an Imperial pen in London, England. An era of pioneers, pugilists and rebels became history. In its place, in 1841, came a new political entity called Canada West, a province that remained in an uneasy union with Canada East until 1867. The next 40 years can best be described in the words of author William Kilbourn: "At a slow summer pace, the land began a century's growth of elms and fat barns and Holsteins, of caution and sobriety and decency."

It was time for a change. The prominent people of the area were growing old. John McDougall, who once sold whisky from his log cabin, was gone. His son was now 65 and retained only a corner of the original farm. Jonathan Hale had split his 400-acre holdings and faded from the scene. James Price had sold "Castlefield" and moved to

Toronto. It was said that he was bankrupted as a result of his financial support of William Lyon Mackenzie. It is true that he held some of Mackenzie's IOU's, but it is unlikely that this caused him much distress. After all, he had bought "Castlefield" for 1,000 pounds, sold it a few years later at nearly 200-percent profit, then bought the next lot to the south for 3,000 pounds. There is no record of bankruptcy. No one need feel sorry for the Honourable James Hervey Price.

Jesse Ketchum began to wind down his holdings. He sold lots on Yonge north of Blythwood from Lot 3, and other parts of Lot 3, to John Boyd and William Cawthra. He left his son, William, to subdivide what is now Blythwood Road. In 1845, at the age of 64, he moved to Buffalo, leaving his remaining North Toronto property to his daughter Fidelia and her husband, the Reverend James Harris. It remained in their hands for many years and was known as "the Harris Farm." It ran from just north of Blythwood to Dawlish Avenue, and from Yonge to Bayview. Fidelia is commemorated in the short street named for her in Lawrence Park. There was also a street named after Jesse Ketchum nearby, but this name was changed to Pinedale Road in the 1940s. Pity!

Earlier in North Toronto's history, there had been a small influx of immigrants from the West Indies. No one knows why well-to-do families from the West Indies migrated to this part of Yonge Street, but they did. The earliest was John Mills Jackson from the island of St. Vincent, but he stayed only long enough to build an estate at Heath and Yonge in 1806.

In 1832 the British Parliament abolished slavery throughout the Empire. The owners of slaves were compensated by government grants, and many such families simply left their West Indian plantations. Samuel Ames Huson was a wealthy gentleman with property in County Kilkenny, Ireland, as well as plantations in Barbados. Huson brought his family to Upper Canada in 1836. Huson was not a frugal man. He chose the most dramatic site in our area, the crown of the hill that is now Lawrence Park. He also chose John Howard, Toronto's most notable architect, to design and build his new home, "Kingsland." The resulting house was reached from Yonge by a bridge and a drive up what is now Lympstone Avenue.

A family from the Barbados, the Murrays, moved into the Glengrove area. They are said to have sheltered John Montgomery's family during the Rebellion. John George Nanton from St. Vincent also moved into the Glengrove area, calling his property "Pilgrim Farm." The Nantons moved into an existing house, probably the old McDougall homestead, and shortly after engaged architect John Howard, who wrote that he was busy making "plans and specs for altering a villa on Yonge Street for Mr. Nanton."

The Husons, Murrays and Nantons fitted easily into the social life of the Toronto area. John Nanton married Louisa Jarvis of the well-known Toronto family. "Kingsland" was the setting for three Huson weddings. In 1840 Ellen Huson married George Shaw, grandson of General Aeneas Shaw of "Oak Hill." In 1842 Georgina Huson married Samuel Bickerton Harman, formerly of Barbados. Harman was to become Mayor of Toronto and later City Treasurer. In 1844 Mary Anne Huson married Davidson Munro Murray from just across Yonge Street. This family produced a succession of notable

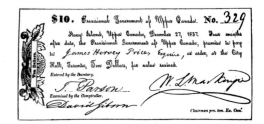

One of Mackenzie's IOU's to James Hervey Price Esquire dated December 27, 1837, and stating that $10 would be paid in four months.

The William Drummond house just south of Bloor and Yonge was built about the same time as "KINGSLAND" and was similar in architectural style, featuring "circular ends."

Toronto lawyers, starting with their son, Huson Murray.

Think back a century and a half to those weddings. Down the long drive from "Kingsland" would come at least three spotless open coaches, the horses shining, the harness gleaming and jingling. In the first coach would be the family — ladies in incredible furbelows, the gentlemen in formal coats and great stovepipe hats. In the second coach would be the bride and her attendants, excited and laughing, resplendent in new gowns (though not in wedding white, that came later). And in the third coach would come the servants, almost members of the family for the day.

"Kingsland" seems to have been very successful in promoting matrimony. When the estate later was sold to William Vance, three of *his* daughters, one at a time, took the happy coach ride down Yonge Street to be married in St. James'.

Meanwhile, North Toronto continued its main business, farming. It was a successful and stable community. In 1842 there were about 20 farms between Eglinton and Deloraine. Thirty-five years later, 13 of these 20 farms were still in the hands of the same families.

These are the families that set the tone of the community in the mid-Victorian years. To this list should be added the Joneses from Bayview, the Mulhollands from Bathurst, and the Moores from Yonge and Eglinton.

Robert Jones came to the area in 1817 and cleared a farm on what is now Bayview Avenue, just south of Lawrence. He and his wife, Mary (Wheelock), became prominent members of the community, and for 90 years the Jones family sent sons and daughters out to the world from that comfortable farm.

The Robert Jones family consisted of six boys and four girls, and they give us some idea of what could become of a large family at that time. Three boys grew up and left home for far places: Samuel to San Francisco and the gold rush; James to Cincinnati, there to die young; and Richard, whom we can't trace. Another son, Robert, stayed on the farm until 1904; William bought and farmed property near Hogg's Hollow; Benjamin, who seemed to have adequate resources, lived on Victoria Avenue for many years, and his widow remained there until the 1920s. One of the girls, May, stayed on the farm, and the other three — Eliza, Henrietta and Fidelia — married local men. Old Robert died at the age of 94. We know the life spans of four of his ten children: they reached 80, 82, 84 and 85 years.

The Jones family was instrumental in having Victoria Avenue (now Blythwood) improved and put through from Yonge to Bayview. Completed by the 1860s, this was one of the first public roads, other than concession lines, in the North Toronto area.

The Moore family acquired, piece by piece, most of the 200-acre lot at the southeast corner of Eglinton and Yonge. After some 40 years the property began to slip away, again piece by piece.

Charles Moore was born in Ireland in 1793, and he was thought to be connected to the Earls of Drogheda, whose family name was Moore. Charles and his wife moved to Newbury on the Hudson River in New York State. However, they found the post-revolutionary attitude not to their liking, so they moved north to Canada.

FAMILY FARMS IN NORTH TORONTO IN 1855

FAMILY	FARM LOCATION
Snyders	Eglinton to Broadway
Bond	Erskine to Keewatin (but lived at Chatsworth and Yonge)
Boyd	Sheldrake, Sherwood
Harris	Blythwood to Dawlish
Lawrence	Lawrence north to Ranleigh, and later south to Dawlish
Easton	Ranleigh to Glenforest
Brooke	Glenforest to Snowdon
Ward	St. Clements to Briar Hill
Jackes	Roselawn to Castlefield
Snyder	Lytton, Alexandra
Hill	Chatsworth to Lawrence
Nightingale	Cranbrooke to Brookdale
Shaw	Brookdale to Fairlawn

These are the families that set the tone of the community in the mid-Victorian years. To this list should be added the Joneses from Bayview, the Mulhollands from Bathurst, and the Moores from Yonge and Eglinton.

Although Irish, the Moores were strong Anglicans and Loyalists. According to one report, "Mr. Moore experienced the difference between the conduct of the Americans and the British in a striking manner as soon as they put foot on Canadian soil. They were hailed with joy by the officers and soldiers there, and they would not allow him to put his hands to remove his effects, but did it themselves, being so delighted to see a British subject coming from the States." (Since most of the people in Upper Canada at the time came from or by way of the States, the "officer and soldiers" must have found it quite exhausting to be hailing each new arrival with joy and physical assistance.)

The Moores were good neighbours and farmers. They built a fine home, "Moore Place," on Yonge south of Eglinton. Some of their eight children might have had the best view of the battle of Montgomery's Tavern, since it was almost directly across Yonge Street from them.

In 1839 Charles Moore became the first People's Warden of St. John's, York Mills. The Moores were close friends of Bishop Strachan, and it may well have been his influence which led them to take part in the founding of St. Paul's Church in Yorkville in 1842.

By 1860 Moore had begun to sell off parts of his farm. Part of the property near Bayview was sold to his 23-year-old son, Erwin. Charles Moore died in 1870 and his wife and one daughter died five years later. The two remaining daughters could not maintain the estate, and they sold the south side of Eglinton, now comprising the 14 short streets that run south from Eglinton between Yonge and Bayview. It was a sad moment for them, and James Lesslie's diary records that the sisters took a trip to the West Indies to recover. On their return, they moved down to 729 Ontario Street, where they could be closer to their church. A nephew, Thomas, took over the house. He was probably the publisher of the *York Gazette* at the time. There were nine in the Thomas Moore family, so the house had a happy resurgence.

The Sniders, or Snyders (spelling was interchangeable in the early years), of Yonge Street continued to prosper and to expand. The original farmstead remained in their hands for at least 65 years. By 1846 Sniders owned three other separate farms in the immediate area, and through marriage, Snider women ran the households of many other homes and farms in the area. The family spread out. For example, Martin's grandson Thomas Albert, like James Jones, went to Cincinnati, which was the departure point for the Mississippi and the opening American West. Others moved to western Canada. Herbert Elgin Snider has put together a genealogy of the Sniders, including the names of some 1,150 descendants of Martin Snyder! The marble memorials to members of this

"MOORE PLACE" stood on the east side of Yonge just north of Soudan. This 1878 drawing shows a house of considerable dignity with ornamental trees, a well-cut lawn, and the fashionable elaborate wooden fence.

family rise tall and stately on the edge of a ravine in Mount Pleasant Cemetery.

The Lawrences also flourished. Peter Lawrence had owned a small tannery at the southwest corner of Lawrence and Yonge in the 1820s. His son William and other members of the family acquired 200 acres northeast of Lawrence and Yonge, and 200 acres northwest of Lawrence and Yonge. William married Emma Fidelia Harris, a granddaughter of Jesse Ketchum. In 1865, at the age of 34, William bought Lot 5 at the southeast corner of Lawrence and Yonge, the biggest part of the present Lawrence Park, including the house built for Samuel Ames Huson 30 years earlier. By the late 1860s the Lawrence farm and the Harris farm were side by side, running from Blythwood to Lawrence and from Yonge to Bayview. One-half of this was owned by William Lawrence; the

The Davisville Methodist Church on Yonge opposite Belsize Drive. This style, a combination of red and yellow brick, was common in Southern Ontario but quite uncommon elsewhere.

other half would be inherited by his wife.

George Sheldon Ward was the founder of another notable North Toronto family. Sheldon Ward, so called to distinguish him from his son George, was born in Toronto and became a carpenter. In 1829 he bought a small lot near Glencairn and Yonge, and in 1832 his was one of the names on the deed for the property for the new Methodist Church.

In 1842 he bought the north half of the old Ruggles farm from J.H. Price. This farm ran from "Castlefield" to Briar Hill and from Yonge almost to Bathurst. The farmhouse was on the south side of what is now St. Clements Avenue, but there is some uncertainty as to whether it was close to Yonge or back almost to Rosewell. In 1989 Allan and Archie Ramsay, surviving nephews-in-law, had different memories as to where the house stood. We do know that the Wards provided the site for the first school to be built in the Eglinton area.

George and Leonora Ward had 11 children between 1851 and 1875. Today's Ramsay family recall an old Ward family saying that "four in the west is thriftier than eleven in the east." George Ward acted on this saying. In 1882 he took four of his older children, one young woman and three young men, to Pheasant Forks, North-West Territories. They travelled in horse-drawn wagons and he helped them buy property and stayed with them for the first year. One of the boys lived to the age of 102. Another, Albert, married Dinah Taylor from Bracebridge, Ontario, and fathered a family of ten children. As of 1990 members of the Ward family are doing well in Lemberg and Porcupine Plain, Saskatchewan.

The youngest member of the family was Mabel Ward (1875-1971). She married William Read Ramsay and they lived at 317 Sheldrake Boulevard, now the home of their son, Allan Ramsay.

The Ward farm provided the site for St. Clement's Anglican Church, St. Clement's School, and Eglinton Presbyterian Church, which became the North Toronto Library and is now a day nursery.

These were the golden years of farming on Yonge Street. Wheat was the most important crop, much of it being exported to the eastern seaboard of the United States, at first by way of the Erie Canal and later by railway. In 1854 the governments of Canada and the United States signed a Free Trade agreement, although they called it, more accurately, "Reciprocity." In five years Canadian exports to the United States increased by 280 percent. But 12 years later the deal was called off, or "abrogated" to use the official term.

Wood was also a valuable crop. If, like the Lawrences, Joneses and McDougalls, you had a sawmill in the Don Valley, you could sell lumber. If not, you could cut and chop firewood for the stoves of Toronto. In the winter horse-drawn sleighs went jingling down to the city, piled high with this valuable cash crop. Hay and oats were also in demand to supply the increasing number of livery stables in Toronto.

Toronto was growing rapidly. In 20 years (1831-1851) the population increased sevenfold to some 30,000. By mid-century there were 21 churches, 51 schools, and 142 inns or taverns! Main streets were lighted by gas. Water mains were laid, but for firefight-

These early houses, 2084 and 2090 Yonge Street, were located between Lola and Manor roads. They could have been the homes of workers from the Davisville Pottery. The "radial" and other street traffic passed by very close to their front doors.

ing only, not for cooking or washing or sewage. Wooden sidewalks ran up Yonge as far as Bloor and were heading for St. Clair. Handsome buildings like Osgoode Hall and St. Michael's Cathedral rose amid houses whose backyards held apple and plum orchards.

Not everyone living on Yonge Street was engaged in farming. South from Eglinton to the present Mt. Pleasant Cemetery, Yonge Street cut diagonally across the usual lot system and invited small holdings. One such lot, No. 17, remained a part of the Clergy Reserves and could only be leased, not owned, until 1911. Further south, the Davis family had taken over the pottery works and were more interested in manufacturing than in farming. People who walked up Yonge Street — and there were many who did — would still avoid the cemetery hollow by walking up what is now Lawton Boulevard and crossing Mud Creek by the milldam.

According to directories of York Township, the population of this area of Yonge Street doubled in the five years from 1846-1851. Little knots of dwellings arose on Yonge Street.

There were small houses on the west side in the Lola-Imperial area, probably built for workers in the pottery or mill. Another group of houses formed when small lots were sold between Broadway and Sherwood. One of the first buildings there was Anthony Smith's blacksmith shop. Other names that would become familiar were introduced here in the 1840s: Weir, Stibbard, Mitchell, Hargrave.

In contrast to the houses above, the KEITH house stood on the west side of Yonge just north of Lawrence. It was probably built in the late 1830s and is similar in style to the Snyder house built in 1828.

There were two small buildings just about at Glencairn, and a little collection of old houses on the east side of Yonge, close to Golfdale. These had been built as early as 1817, probably for people who worked for Seneca Ketchum in his store across the street.

By the 1840s and 1850s almost every house was built to a traditional style, a central door flanked by a window or two on either side. If a second storey was added, it simply meant repeating this pattern, or perhaps adding just a dormer window above the door. Even the slope of the roof was standardized. The "Keith house," which stood just north of Lawrence on the west side of Yonge, is a good example.

The most fashionable building material was brick. A good, comfortable brick home was the ideal, but there were other building methods. The frame house, sometimes clapboard over an original log cabin, or simply a wood-framed clapboard house, was more common and cheaper than brick. In 1842 John Ross advertised that he would build houses of unburnt brick, and he built such a house on Yonge just north of Blythwood. William Ramsay and William Hill built similar houses in the same location.

This unburnt or "mud-brick" house was well suited to the climate, since it provided a wall at least 18 inches thick with good insulation properties. By 1855 a magazine noted that "there are…many country residences of this description in the country to the north of Toronto." There was also the Pise method of construction, in which earth was rammed between board walls 18 inches apart, after which the boards could be removed and used again as a form. This anticipated the current system of poured concrete. The durability of mud-brick houses was astonishing. In 1937 it was a difficult job to tear down one such house, the old Ramsay house at Blythwood and Yonge.

In the 1820s, to live on Yonge Street was to live on the edge of the wilderness. Connection with the rest of the world was difficult, slow and expensive. Mail delivery could take weeks. News was equally slow — news of the Battle of Waterloo took nearly three months to reach York. To bring even one cherished piece of furniture from your original home took a great deal of time and trouble. The coming of steamboats to Lake Ontario helped, but it was still a long and tedious journey anywhere beyond the lake ports.

All that changed in the next 30 years. It was not just that Yonge Street was macadamized; the whole world of travel changed. Stagecoaches began to run on schedule and with reasonable comfort. Mails were accelerated.

In the 1850s, suddenly there were railways. It is difficult for us to comprehend the stunning effect of the coming of the railway. In all of previous history no one had ever been able to travel faster than a galloping horse. Now, abruptly, in little provincial Canada West, you could go 300 miles in one day instead of the 15 uncomfortable miles that you had hitherto counted on. By the mid-1850s the Grand Trunk Railway connected Toronto with Sarnia on the west and with Montreal on the east. New York could be reached through Buffalo. The Northern Railway did not go up Yonge Street — too many hills and valleys — but it now provided a route up to Newmarket, Lake Simcoe, and even Georgian Bay.

Yonge Street people, hearing the unforgettable steam whistle of the Northern, certainly realized that they were no longer isolated, but very much a part of a new, interconnected world. It meant a new view of the world. Thackeray, whose popular books were available in Toronto, wrote: "We who lived before railways...are like Father Noah and his family out of the Ark."

Farming also changed. Where farmers had hitherto been clearing fields and learning to cope with the Yonge Street winters and soils, now there was time for, and interest in, the "science of farming." Practical incentive came from a local man. William McDougall, born and raised on a farm at Glengrove and Yonge, started a journal called the *Canadian Agriculturalist* in the 1840s. It was a remarkably sophisticated and, for its day, scientific publication. Articles were reprinted from the United States and Britain, as well as letters and essays from local people. George Leslie, of Leslie Street, wrote a long article on ornamental trees suitable for our area. Another writer discussed the area's suitability for eight distinct species of turnip, including "the yellow, or Ruta Baga."

McDougall's journal helped to promote local agricultural events. There were plowing matches, where the new steel plow (called the "singing plow" because it vibrated with a musical tone as it turned the furrow) demonstrated its ability to shed even the stickiest clay. There were annual agricultural fairs, which included contests for just about every kind of animal and farm product. In the 1850 fair, the wax flowers of Miss Elliott of Yonge Street gained much admiration. John Davis customarily won the award

THE YONGE STREET FARMS

At William McDougall's invitation, Mr. Robinson, the editor of the authoritative U.S. Agriculturalist, *came to Yonge Street in 1850. Here is his description, in part:*

FARMS of 200 acres with a good comfortable brick house and outbuildings, and good barn, well fenced...averaging 25 bushels of wheat, and 30 or 40 bushels of oats, and 200 of potatoes, will sell for $50 an acre along Yonge Street...there are few cattle, but several flocks of fine sheep.

I count a greater proportion of good substantial real serviceable farm horses here upon this road than upon any other that I have travelled.

for the best pottery. The Reverend James Harris and Mr. Silas Snider lived across from one another on Yonge Street, and both had entries in the apples and pears categories. The judges were unable, or unwilling, to declare a winner, so they declared a tie in three categories.

Farm outbuildings were more important than farmhouses, perhaps as an assertion of male authority. As late as 1880, 54 percent of Yonge Street farm buildings were assessed as being of "first quality," while only 45 percent of farmhouses were so described. But the *Canadian Agriculturalist* had definite thoughts even on farmhouses: "The interior of a house should always be painted of a warm, neutral tint. Pure white is too cold and cheerless...." And as to the exterior, "the colours and tints proper for home painting...are browns, drabs, yellows, pea green, grays...."

Some early mechanical farm implements were available in the 1830s, but in the 1850s they came in a flood. The horse-drawn mowing machine was first to be generally accepted. These were made by a number of small local companies. The addition of the mechanical reaper a few years later changed farming forever. Up to that time a man with a scythe could cut about one acre of wheat in a day. This limited the amount of wheat that could be grown, since there was a crucial ten-day harvesting period. Now the farmer could plant more, confident in his ability to harvest his crop.

The mechanical reaper and binder increased a man's productivity in the fields tenfold.

Perhaps the best indication of change came in the sudden emergence of a new occupation, that of mechanic. If there are farm machines, then there must be people capable of maintaining them. On this part of Yonge Street in 1866, one out of every six persons in the Directory called himself a mechanic. This completely new occupation is surely similar to the sudden burst of computer programmers a century later.

Even women were finding life a little easier. In 1847 York By-Law 134 authorized the establishment of a school that girls could attend.

Dramatic changes were taking place in the Victorian house. Pioneer wives had cooked under unbelievably primitive conditions — no stove, no sink, and certainly no refrigerator. But by the 1830s cast-iron stoves were coming into use, a great change from pots hanging from hooks over a fire. Some houses even had a sink of sorts. Water had to be carried pail by pail from the well, but you might be fortunate enough to have a drain that ran the water out through the wall and into the ground. It was no longer necessary to make your own soap by a laborious combination of lye and fats, as soap could now be bought quite inexpensively.

The woman of the house still had to make her own clothing, and that of her husband and children, but by the 1850s some ready-made clothing was being manufactured in Toronto and Berlin (Kitchener). More practical help came in the 1850s, when the sewing machine came into use — thanks to the million-dollar advertising campaign of Isaac M. Singer, who prospered, retired to England, and left an estate of $13,000,000 (the actual inventor of the sewing machine was Walter Hunt, who destroyed his machines and patents because he feared they would put seamstresses out of work).

In 1854 a Canadian doctor named Abraham Gasner developed and patented kerosene, a cheap substitute for the whale oil that had made lamps too expensive for most households. Through the mid-1800s other helpful devices came on the market. These included apple-peelers, sausage-stuffers, safety pins, and washboards. An important boost to womanhood came with the publication of Isabella Beeton's *Book of Household Management*. Science and social correctness gave some dignity to the housewife. *Rose-Belfords Canadian Monthly* was a popular magazine in the Toronto area. By 1878 some very modern thoughts on women were being aired: "A thorough and systematic education is more and more admitted to be the natural right of girls as well as their brothers — and within certain limits, which are daily widening, it is more and more fully conceded that whatever women know they can do, they have a right to do...In Canada we are liberal...Queen's University already being declared open to ladies." Articles of this kind were frequently read in the journals of the time.

Most Upper Canadians had previously considered education to be simply a frill. Even as late as the 1850s, only one half of the school-age children spent as much as one year at school. But life on Yonge Street was changing. In the 1850s there was a wave of expansion in the paper industry and the printed word. Farmers needed to be able to read technical farming journals. Their sons wanted to read about the new West, or perhaps how to become railway men or telegraph operators. Many people simply wanted to read novels, like those of Charles Dickens, as serialized in Toronto papers. There was rush to education, but there was a move in that direction. Twenty years later (1870), children spent three times longer in school.

The first school in the Eglinton area was built in 1842 on a lot severed from the Ward farm, just south of the present St. Clements Avenue. Fifty years later, in 1892, the *Recorder* reminisced about "a log schoolhouse...situated some hundred yards south (of the Methodist Church) on the opposite side of Yonge...the first class meeting being held by a Mr. William Wheelock...." Perhaps we can assume that Mr. Wheelock was the first teacher, and that he may have been a relative, perhaps a brother, to the Mary Wheelock who married Robert Jones of Bayview.

In 1845 John Boyd, age 45, came up from Toronto to teach at the Eglinton school. He was a graduate of the Bay Street Academy, a somewhat upper-class school under the patronage of men like Robert Baldwin and Bishop Strachan. His work was promising enough to give him a teaching position at the Academy. He came to the Eglinton area partly because he had just bought a farm in the area of the present Sheldrake Boulevard. John Boyd could simply walk across Yonge Street to the school, while running his farm outside of school hours. He and his wife, Margaret, had one child, who would have had to commute to Toronto to continue his education. Dr. Henry Scadding speaks of Eglinton's young people, "who some years ago used to be seen twice every day at all seasons, travelling between that place and Toronto, rising early and late taking rest in order to be punctually present at and carefully ready for classroom and lecture-room in town."

Boyd's teaching was highly successful, at least in the case of his son, John Alexander Boyd, who was to have a distinguished legal career, including 25 years as Chancellor of Ontario, the justice presiding over the Courts of Chancery. And his grandson, Alexander James Boyd, was to be famous in more robust fields. He became captain of the Argonaut

The EGLINTON POST OFFICE opened in 1858 and was operated by Miss Hattie Hargrave. It stood on the east side of Yonge just north of Keewatin. It also served as a small store and the home of the Hargrave family.

Rowing Club and a member of the Dominion Champion Football Club. He also went to the Northwest Rebellion with the Queen's Own Regiment, and then on to the Boer War with Strathcona's Horse, a noted cavalry unit.

As the population increased and school became more popular, three more schools were built: one on the southeast corner of Bathurst and Glencairn (1864); one on the northeast corner of Bayview and Eglinton; and a third (1860) at Davisville, just east of Yonge. The latter was a two-room school, and it is said to have drawn pupils from Leaside and from as far away as Lawrence Avenue. It perhaps offered a year or two of further schooling.

Yonge Street had become a good address. In 1844 William Augustus Baldwin had a large house built in Deer Park. In the same year, his architect, John Howard, drove his family up as far as York Mills to show them the sights, including the three or four houses he had designed or modified in the area. By 1850 Howard was bringing his friends to watch the "pigeon shoot" at Finch's Hotel. In the 1840s and 1850s the sky would literally be darkened each spring and fall by the flights of many millions of passenger pigeons, which could not only be shot, but even killed with clubs.

Social amenities increased. In 1853 a doctor came to live in Eglinton. He was 30 years old and had the resounding name of Orlando Salathiel Winstanley. (In the 1866 Directory of York Township, Dr. Winstanley's occupation is listed as "butcher." It would seem that someone bore him a grudge!)

In 1858 a post office was opened in Eglinton, on Yonge, almost opposite the present St. Clements Avenue. By 1862 a wooden sidewalk ran from the bay right up Yonge Street as far as Lawrence, and the lines of the Electro-Magnetic Telegraph Company stretched out of sight up Yonge.

In a typically British way, clubs became fashionable. The Agricultural Society was not alone. In 1850 an Orange Lodge was founded, and members met regularly at the Glebe Inn. By 1863 the Order of Masons was established and meeting at the Prospect House in Eglinton. Temperance societies flourished. A YMCA operated on Yonge Street in the 1860s — a YMCA much more concerned with souls than bodies. A public reading room was set up by James Lesslie and others.

In five years (1851-56) the population of Ontario grew by 40 percent and the village of Eglinton shared in this growth. Notable among the newcomers were the Scottish families, the Fishers and the Ramsays, who would have much to do with the growth of Eglinton and later of North Toronto.

Leaving for the new world was often a heart-rending experience. Few of those who left would ever have a chance to return; partings were sad and final. The voyage itself was long and exhausting. William Ramsay, wife Jean, and their family were six weeks in crossing the ocean. One of their three children died at sea. The family settled in Eglinton in 1856. Although he had been a stonemason in Scotland, William, now 44 years of age, adapted to his new environment and he built a mud-brick house for his family on Yonge Street, just north of Blythwood. Eighty years later that mud-brick house gave the wreckers a valiant tussle before it came down. The Ramsays' son, James, living in an area surrounded by sawmills, apprenticed as a carpenter.

The Fishers arrived in Canada one year before the Ramsays, but they first settled as tenants on a Scarborough farm. The father of the family died soon after arrival, leaving John, at 17 years, his mother and one younger brother. Farm life did not appeal to young John, and he also apprenticed to a carpenter.

By 1861 James Ramsay and John Fisher had met and formed the construction company of Fisher and Ramsay. James Lesslie's diary mentions that "Young Fisher" had come around offering to do various jobs that would be beyond the capacity of the retired Lesslie. The diary also mentions "Ramsay," whose wagon was the only one big enough to carry the load of young chestnut trees downtown to be planted on Jesse Ketchum's Temperance Street. The success of these young men and their company will be described in later chapters.

The Family Compact faction had not really come victoriously out of the Rebellion of 1837. Within three years it became clear that the British government was now favouring "responsible government." Responsible government, in its simplest form, meant that the locally *elected* government should no longer be at the mercy of *appointed* officials. This was one of the objectives of the Reformers and was opposed by the Tories.

The fight between Tories and Reformers in the 1840s involved some astonishing political gyrations. For example, a French-Canadian, LaFontaine, was overwhelmingly elected to represent Yonge Street. Robert Baldwin, who didn't speak much French, was joyously "chaired" around the town of Rimouski. And finally, the Reform party, with a huge majority, resigned en masse and left Canada without an elected government for almost an entire year, in 1843 and 1844.

During these years the City of Toronto voted strongly Tory, while Yonge Street and York County voted equally strongly for the Reformers. It stayed that way throughout the Canada West years (1841-1867).

The Eglinton area continued to be a part of the Home District in matters of local affairs. There was a council of the Home District, a vague attempt at local government. Established in 1842, it had little real authority. Franklin Jackes was the council member representing York County. Jackes and James Price, the latter a member of Parliament, worked hard for continuing improvements to York roads. To their surprise, in 1849 the Inspector-General of Canada, Sir Francis Hincks, announced that the roads of York County would be sold. Jackes offered 60,000 pounds on behalf of the Home District council, but this was rejected. A further offer of 75,000 pounds was also turned down.

On August 17, 1850, the public was astonished to hear that Yonge Street and all county roads had been sold privately to Mr. James Beaty of the Toronto Road Company for some 75,000 pounds. The Toronto *Globe* reported: "...of all the numerous cases of executive malversation and actual stealing of public money...the York Road Job is perhaps the most daring and flagitious".

As it turned out Mr. Beaty had not made the best of bargains. Traffic on Yonge Street was dropping because of the railway, and it became popular to complain about the condition of the roads, knowing that the repairs would not affect taxes. Beaty was not unhappy to sell the roads back to the province in 1863, and four years later York County took them over for $72,000. (Note that the selling price was in dollars, while the buying price was in pounds.)

James Beaty moved to Eglinton in 1856, buying up the Nanton property at Glengrove. He had come to York in 1818 and had been successful in the leather business and as the publisher of the *Toronto Leader*. He sold his Eglinton property in 1881 and 1886, but went on to an active but sometimes questionable political life. He became a senator and was semi-affectionately known as "Old Jimmy." He lived to the age of 94.

In 1849 the Baldwin Act took steps to strengthen local government. The Township of York was created, covering the area from the Humber to Scarborough, and from the city north to Steeles Avenue. The logical centre of this area was just north of the present Eglinton Avenue. The Township of York, therefore, took as its headquarters the little village that had come to be known as Eglington. Eglinton or Eglington was apparently named after the 26-year-old Earl of Eglinton, of Ayrshire, Scotland. This energetic and historically-minded young man "announced his intention of holding a full-scale tournament of knights in armour…What might at least have been a colourful spectacle was washed out by the heaviest rainfall in memory, and the affair became a laughing stock, as well as leaving his estate in debt for the rest of his life! Nevertheless, he was admired for his boldness."

The man chosen to head up the new local government was Franklin Jackes. He brought valuable experience to the job, since for the past seven years he had represented the area in the council of the Home District.

Jackes had been a baker in Toronto and had shared the representation of St. David's ward with William Lyon Mackenzie. He moved to Eglinton in 1842 and bought the "Castlefield" estate. Perhaps he continued baking at "Castlefield." As of this writing there are still some very old and unusual ovens in a small building on the west side of Duplex, just north of Roselawn Avenue. These ovens would have been quite close to the back of "Castlefield," which actually extended onto the present Duplex Avenue. The ovens were used later by Harry Hook as part of his candy factory at Duplex and Roselawn, but they were old ovens when he bought the property in the 1920s.

Jackes and his wife had a large family and entertained frequently. "Castlefield" was a busy and well-tended estate. Unfortunately Jackes died from smallpox at the age of 48, just three years after his appointment as the first reeve of York Township and the first warden of York County.

Franklin Jackes, warden of York County, first reeve of York Township, and second owner of the "Castlefield" estate.

In 1851 there was a township council of four men to assist the reeve: William Mulholland from the Bathurst area; William Lea from the future Leaside; William James from east of the Don; and William Tyrrell from Weston. (William was obviously a popular first name, as evidenced from the names of the council members, but none of these Williams was old enough to have been named after King William IV, who bravely gave up his actress mistress to marry a German princess and try, unsuccessfully, to provide an heir to the British throne. More likely, the name William was in honour of William III, the hero of the Orange Order.) John Willson IV was the clerk. Until 1866 the four members of council selected one of their number as reeve. After that date the reeve was elected by vote. Jackes, as the first reeve, was appointed. Incidentally, voting was still done by raising the hand and making a public statement about the candidate endorsed. It was 1874 before voting by secret ballot was introduced. Arguments against the secret ballot were many and vigorous.

Meetings were held in the local hotel at first. There was a real need for accommodation since attendance at a meeting involved an overnight trip for some members of council. Meetings were held "on or before the full of the moon," so that horse and rider would have some visibility on the way home. In the early years the member from east of the Don made his way to below Bloor, crossed the Don at the Winchester Street bridge, and thence over to Yonge and up to Eglinton. Eglinton Avenue was then known as the Base Line, but it was little more than a survey line in some places and was not usually passable, except close to Yonge Street. At first the member from Weston would come across Lawrence Avenue, but by the 1860s William Tyrrel took the train from Weston to Toronto, and then up Yonge by horse-drawn coach.

Eglinton village grew and flourished, and several of its notable citizens merit mention. In 1855 William McDougall (1822-1905) returned to live near the scene of his childhood, where he had played with the Indians who visited the Fox Creek ravine just south of Chatsworth Drive. He had married the adopted, only daughter of the Joseph Eastons, whose farm occupied all of Lot 7 on the east side of Yonge north of Lawrence. Living at that farm, and with the aid of a mortgage from Sandford Fleming — of Standard Time fame — he set up a sawmill in the ravine at the back of the property.

McDougall had attended Victoria College at Cobourg. He had published the *Canadian Agriculturalist* and later a newspaper called the *North American*. For a time he worked as a lawyer in the office of J.H. Price. By the 1850s he was deeply into politics, a handsome, well-spoken man with good connections. Two of his sisters were married to sons of Robert Baldwin, the perennial Premier of the province. Another sister married David Reesor from Markham, who later became a senator.

McDougall helped to found the Clear Grit movement. This political group advocated what were then very radical views, most of which have long since been accepted — vote by ballot, regular elections, etc. He wanted, he said, to "roll the country down to a common-sense democracy." He became one of the Fathers of Confederation and served in the Ontario legislature from 1875 to 1878, and in the federal Parliament from 1878 to 1882. Meanwhile, he developed an independence of mind that did not quite fit with the need for tight party politics. George Brown, when Premier, wrote to a friend, "But who is to be Secretary of the Province? I fear it will have to be Mr. McDougall." His political opponents called him "Wandering Willie" because he changed from Clear Grit to Conservative. In 1869 he was appointed Lieutenant-Governor of the North-West Territories, but he was repulsed by Louis Riel's men, who prevented him from entering the territory he had come to govern. This ended his effective political career.

In 1856 James Metcalfe bought a farm on Yonge running north from Bedford Park Avenue to Fairlawn. Metcalfe was born in England, went to school in Manchester, and trained as a builder in his father's office. In 1841 he arrived in Toronto, and during the next ten years his company built the St. Lawrence Hall, the Post Office on Toronto Street, the Normal School, St. James Cathedral, and old Trinity College. In 1852 he responded to the lure of gold and left for Australia, where he apparently convinced the city fathers of Melbourne that he could repeat his Toronto successes. In the next four years he erected some of the finest buildings in Melbourne — the Public Library, the Bank of New South Wales, the Hall of Commerce, and the London Chartered Bank of Australia.

There is no doubt that Metcalfe was a successful and wealthy man when he came to

WILLIAM MCDOUGALL, was born near Glengrove and Yonge in 1822 and went on to become an important journalist and politician. He also became one of the Fathers of Confederation.

Bedford Park. He set about building a suitable estate, a spacious house surrounded by formal gardens in which exotic birds roamed. There was adequate stabling for horses and pasture land for a herd of prize Holstein cattle.

Metcalfe became the popular and able federal member of Parliament for East York. He was also president of the Royal Canadian Bank in 1866. He and his wife, born Ellen Howson, had one son, who became a Methodist minister. Unfortunately, the Metcalfe house burned down in 1868. It was a discouraging setback, and the Metcalfes moved to Yorkville, where James died in 1886.

In 1856 Thomas Winslow Anderson also came back to the scene of his youth. He had been a rebel running through the woods in the Rebellion of 1837. He had fled to the United States, where he "chopped wood for a few years." His brother, John, had escaped with John Montgomery. Thomas returned to Canada when amnesty was granted in the 1840s, and by 1856 was in a position to buy the old Hill farm, covering the present Chatsworth, Cheritan and Chudleigh area, and running from Yonge to Bathurst.

James Lesslie was a newcomer and an important man in the history of York and Upper Canada. He bought a historic house, the house that John Montgomery built in 1837. The estate consisted of 27 acres of ground, and the house was located in a magnificent position overlooking not only the village of Eglinton, but across to Scarborough and down to where the church steeples of Toronto could just be seen. The house is gone now, but it stood on the west side of Oriole Parkway between present Elwood and Willowbank, overlooking what is now Eglinton Park.

Lesslie had come to Canada with his three brothers — and William Lyon Mackenzie — in the 1820s. By the 1850s he owned a newspaper and a successful stationery business; he was a founding shareholder in a bank and an insurance company; and he owned valuable property in downtown Toronto. But his importance was not due to his wealth. It was his firm and continuing pressure for political reform. He was a man that the Family Compact could neither absorb nor bully. He had been jailed without warrant in 1837. His response was to buy a newspaper and use it to preach reform to a broader audience. Robert Baldwin deserves much credit for obtaining responsible government, but it could not have been obtained without the steady backing of men like Lesslie.

Lesslie operated his 27 Eglinton acres as a working farm, and he took the task seriously. In addition to raising livestock, including peacocks, he planted a good-sized orchard on the eastern slope. It is likely that Orchard View Boulevard takes its name from these orchards, so clearly visible at the end of that street.

Lesslie spent 28 years of happy semi-retirement with his beloved wife, Jacqueline, at "The Willows." In the course of that time the village of Eglinton grew up at his feet. Familiar names run through Lesslie's diary — Mulhollands, Stibbards, John Fisher, and "young" Ramsay.

Lesslie and Jacqueline were active in community affairs. He participated in the establishment of a public reading room in Eglinton, renting for the purpose an old Mulholland house near the corner of Yonge and Eglinton. He helped to found the Eglinton YMCA. Every Friday Jacqueline took the horse and carriage down to the Tor-

JAMES METCALFE, M.P., was the kind of man who creates legends. One popular story is that he went bankrupt and left for Australia, where he made a fortune. He then came back to Yonge Street and entertained his creditors at dinner, placing the money he owed each of them, including interest, under their plates. Unfortunately, this romantic tale is unlikely.

onto jail, where she read the Bible to the inmates. This may sound overly pious today, but it was regarded as helpful in those days. Jacqueline mentioned that it was hardest to read to those who were awaiting execution.

Even in his seventies, Lesslie went downtown several times a week, walking down to Yorkville, taking the tram to King Street, and then returning the same way. By 1862 there was a wooden sidewalk that ran up to Lawrence Avenue. People not only walked a good deal in those days, but sometimes walked quite briskly. Young Larratt Smith walked from King and Yonge to Finch and Yonge in 2 hours and 18 minutes, but he had the grace to pause for a libation at Mr. Finch's Tavern before continuing his walk home to Newmarket.

On one occasion, in January 1877, Lesslie reports that he "got a ride home with Mr. Bescoby." It is an illuminating statement. James Bescoby and James Lesslie had been nearest neighbours across from one another for ten years, yet it is quite possibly that this was one of the few times they spoke to each other. This coldness was the result of events 40 years earlier. James Bescoby came from England with his family in the 1830s. In the 1837 Rebellion, Bescoby was on the side of the Tories and was captain of a party of men in the attack at Montgomery's Tavern. This was the basis for mutual dislike by Lesslie and Bescoby, and for ten years of formality between near neighbours. Today peace has been declared. Lesslie and Bescoby lie 30 feet apart in Mount Pleasant Cemetery.

By 1839 the Bescobys were close friends of architect John Howard and his wife. The two men became business associates in the production of lime for cement. Bescoby became the first man to make Portland cement in Canada. He bought mills and properties at Limehouse in Halton County, and he produced the cement that was used in the construction of the big new asylum at 999 Queen Street West. In 1844 John Howard "surveyed and constructed a small railway into the limestone quarry on the east side of Yonge Street for Mr. Edward Bescoby — the quarry belonged to Charles Thompson." This would be on the "Summerhill" estate on the side of the hill south of St. Clair.

In 1845, according to the *Historical Atlas of York County*, the Bescobys moved to Eglinton, building a comfortable home on the south side of Eglinton, closer to Braemar than to Elmsthorpe.

By 1867 there was clearly a village of Eglinton, with all the services that a village required. There was a church, a school and a post office. Add to these a hotel, a doctor, merchant, butcher, blacksmith and, for variety, a "whipmaker." There were perhaps 20 houses, and most of them would have had a vegetable garden and a small orchard. Even flower gardens were appearing, although only "Castlefield" maintained a full-time gardener.

At "Castlefield" the future Dr. George W. Jackes was 16 years old. He was probably quite unaware of the gardens, but perhaps fully aware of Almira Jane Snyder from just up the street, the woman whom he would later marry. Almira's home would likely still have been one storey, but perhaps it had the surrounding verandah, so that old Martin Snyder could watch the world go by and reminisce about his wives, Alida (d.1837) and Abigail (d.1853). He could smile as he thought of his successful years and of his children

The Guinness Book of World Records *might note that JAMES BESCOBY moved to Eglinton in 1845 as a mature man, yet his wife was still living in the same house in 1931 – eighty-six years later. (She was, as you may have guessed his second wife.)*

who now owned five local farms.

Eglinton in 1867 was just two generations removed from its pioneers. William Snyder was one of the last who could remember the primeval forest from which the rich countryside had emerged. But the golden years were almost over. •

THE POST-CONFEDERATION YEARS

1800   *1820*   *1840*

1855   *1865*

1875   *1880*

*By the 1860s the crinoline and the
hoop-skirt had made the female figure
into a stucture; only a vivid imagination
could detect the shape of the body from the
waist down. For a short period even the
legs of tables and pianos were discreetly
concealed by lace coverings.*

IT WAS a day of "public bonfires, ox roasting, military drills, lake excursions, and at evening, fireworks, while Chinese lanterns lit the trees of Queen's Park in softly glowing colours," wrote historian J.M.S. Careless. Thus, Toronto celebrated Confederation on July 1, 1867. We can be sure that Yonge Street sparkled with lanterns that night as people made their way home through the little villages of Deer Park, Davisville and Eglinton.

Confederation had brought together some four million "British Americans" into one Dominion, and the future looked bright. (Most Québécois would hardly agree to the term "British Americans," but it was a term commonly used in English-language journalism of the day.) Not only newspapers, but church, farm and business journals were filled with "the British Empire" and "Progress."

One of the strongest symbols of that Empire was Queen Victoria herself. Generations of Canadians responded to her belief in family, loyalty and respectability. Family was an easy ideal for Yonge Streeters, as local society was already based on large intermarried families. Loyalty was important because Eglinton was the administrative centre of York Township. When Prince Arthur passed through the edge of the township by train, an effusive message of welcome was drawn up at Eglinton and presented, with suitable bows, at Weston. Respectability was a keynote of the times and involved a series of rules of behaviour. Many of these rules were laid out in books like Mrs. Beeton's *Book of Household Management*. This book gave firm and broad-ranging instructions to the "solidly respectable woman."

There were innumerable rules and conventions. Sometimes rules were iron-clad. For those who were invited to a reception for the Princess Louise in Toronto in 1879 — and probably some of the Jackes would have been included — the invitation was accompanied by these firm instructions: "Ladies are to wear low-necked dresses...Ladies whose health will not admit of their wearing low-necked dresses may, on forwarding to the Aide-de-Camp-in-Waiting a medical certificate to that effect, wear square-cut dresses. Dresses fastening up to the throat may not be worn."

The Pond, Mount Pleasant Cemetery, Toronto, Canada

In the 1870s Mount Pleasant Cemetery was planned and the land was bought. The first internments took place in 1876. This postcard depicting the cemetery's pond was sent to the U.S. on October 7, 1910 for the cost of 1 cent.

The author's father recalled that, with other lads from Deer Park, he defied the ghosts and cold water for a midnight swim – and poached duck eggs at the same time.

Fashion flowed from London to the colonies, reaching Yonge Street very quickly. Working clothes for women had changed very little from those shown on page 24, but for church and social occasions, clothing was much more elaborate. Opinion varied as to the comfort of the hoop skirt. "Oh, it was delightful!" Aunt Etty said. "I've never been so comfortable…It kept your petticoats away from your legs and made walking so light and easy." Not everyone agreed: "To walk with so immense a paraphernalia around one was not easy…To be able to sit required a miracle of precision."

The hoop skirt of the 1850s billowed out in all directions in what was called the "tea-cosy" look. But by the 1860s there was a change. The skirt still billowed out at the back, but fell straight at the front. This effect was achieved by means of a structure made of whalebone, wire and horsehair. Skirts were floor-length throughout the nineteenth century. "Walking the streets trailing clouds of dust was horrible," said one woman. "I once found I had carried into the house a banana skin which had got caught up in the unstitched hem of my dress." But fashion ruled. On Yonge Street, most women would have owned at least one good costume, as countless old family photographs show.

If the reader is searching for the "good old days," perhaps the time to investigate is the 1870s and 1880s. There were big, bustling families where everyone's chores fitted into a common rhythm. Life was close to nature and its four Ontario seasons. There was intellectual stimulation available from journals, and local lectures and discussions, and fairly easy access to dramatic and musical fare in Toronto. Of course, it was a simple horse-and-buggy society, and people worked long, hard hours, but perhaps they were none the worse off for being kept busy. Some women spent lives in misery through

MRS. BEETON'S
Book of Household Management

A typical excerpt follows:
"A Mistress should rise at *latest* at seven o'clock. This will appear dreadfully late to some notables, but will be found to be a good hour *all year round*. The mistress should take her cold bath, and perform a neat, careful, and pretty morning toilet. Having performed this careful toilet, she will be ready to descend at eight o'clock, but before leaving her room, will place two chairs at the end of the bed, and turn the whole of the bedclothes over them; and, except for very rainy mornings, will throw open the windows of her room…

"…The use of cosmetics is a positive breach of sincerity…It is acting a lie to all intents and purposes, and it ought to be held in the same kind of detestation as falsehood with the tongue."

69

successive pregnancies; others revelled in it. On average, it was a healthy and productive society for most people. The warmth of the big, busy kitchen and the sound of sleigh bells formed happy memories for many early North Torontonians.

In the 1870s the farm fields north of Toronto ripened as serenely as usual, but they were not as golden as they had been in the 1850s. Now the wheat crop alternated with oats, corn or a second crop of hay. Throughout Southern Ontario, farming was changing from a specialization in wheat to more general farming.

The early 1870s were a time of depression in Ontario. Trade with the United States was reduced when the U.S. cancelled the free trade, or "reciprocity," policy that had been in effect for some 12 years. At the same time, Ontario wheat was getting serious competition from the western U.S. producers, and even from the Canadian West. From his Eglinton farm, George Ward had seen the change coming. He made sure that 4 of his 11 children moved to the Canadian West. By 1882 Manitoba had boomed to a population of 150,000.

Cows at milking time on their way to Bryce's Dairy. The well-used cowpath would, in a few years, become Alexandra Boulevard.

There were many other opportunities for local farmers. Toronto was growing rapidly and offered a nearby and steady market for farm products. William Davies' meat packing plant on the lower Don River had 3,000 employees by 1867, and it consumed a tremendous amount of cattle and hogs. Bacon and pork, either smoked or packed in ice, became a major export and may have given Toronto its nickname of "Hogtown." There was a market for live cattle in both Britain and the United States. Robert Cook of Eglinton shipped "fine cattle for the markets of London and Aberdeen." The outbuildings of the Lawrence farm look very much like cattle barns, and we know that a very valuable bull "with brass-tipped horns" was stolen from Frank Lawrence. Horses were also a valuable commodity. Horses fed on hay and oats were considered to be stronger than American corn-fed horses, and many were exported to Pennsylvania. Hay, straw and firewood were in constant demand in Toronto.

Milk and poultry also found a market in the city. "Old Jimmy" Beaty sold one-half of his Glengrove farm to the Toronto Dairy Company. The original Snyder farm (at Lytton) was sold and became known as Bryce's Dairy and later as the Toronto Hygienic Dairy Company. In the 1890s Eden Farms, on Bayview north of Eglinton, maintained a large dairy herd. The Toronto Poultry and Garden Produce Company operated as a wholesaler on the south side of Eglinton. Market gardens and greenhouse keepers began to move up from the city. George Plumb's greenhouse at Davisville was one of the first.

But Toronto was much more than a market. In the 20 years after 1873, the rural area around Eglinton became suburban. The city reached out, in author Eric Arthur's words, "always with green fields and singing birds beyond, and seeds of decay behind."

In those 20 years no fewer than 21 major blocks of land changed hands, covering by far the greater part of the district. In most cases the buyers were investors or developers. The earliest developments had been back in the 1850s. At that time Jesse Ketchum's son, William, had opened up part of Victoria Avenue (now Blythwood Road) and the adjacent parts of Yonge Street to builders. The Hon. James Price sold the north side of Eglinton West in ten-acre lots before retiring to England in 1860. A plan for subdivision of what is now Davisville Avenue was approved in 1858.

In 1873 and '74 York Township approved three more major plans of subdivision. Plan 334 opened up Montgomery Avenue and adjacent Yonge Street. Plan 356 created Merton Street and Balliol Avenue. At Eglinton and Yonge, subdivision of the Moore farm opened Soudan and Hillsdale avenues, and also the short streets running south from Eglinton to Soudan.

It was a busy time for the York Township Council. They met in the Eglinton Masonic Hall, which was just north of the Prospect House hotel, at what is now Montgomery and Yonge. The members of council would break for lunch at the hotel next door. Most of them would have brought oats in their wagons, and the hostler would see

In 1874 a Masonic Hall was built on the northwest corner of Yonge and Montgomery. The first floor was rented to the Township of York. Fire destroyed the building in 1881, and the township bought the "lot and ruins." A new Town Hall was built, and this picture shows the Masons meeting in a second-floor hall they rented from the township. In 1909 a separate Masonic Hall was opened on Yonge below Eglinton.

that the horses were fed and watered.

In the last chapter we noted the number of men named William and assumed from this some association with the Orange Order. In the 1870s there was an even more obvious connection with the Masonic Order. The clerk-treasurer of York Township was also the secretary-treasurer of the York Masonic Hall Company, where the council met. In 1877 there was some discussion about the township buying the Masonic Hall, but the sale did not go through — the combined secretaries being unable to agree with himself!

In 1880 the chummy liaison between the Masons and the township was simply turned upside down. The Masonic Hall and Prospect House burned to the ground. For almost two years the council met at Brunskill's Hotel in Davisville, while the council rented offices in the YMCA. Then the council bought the burned-out site of the Masonic Hall and built a new Town Hall. The firm of Fisher and Ramsay completed the building by 1884. Now the Masons rented from the township, instead of the township renting from the Masons.

The treasurer of the York Township Council, and also of the York Masonic Hall Company, was Arthur Lawrence Willson. A second-generation descendant of John Willson, of the eighteenth-century King's Mill on the Humber, and a nephew of Stillwell Willson, of early Yonge Street days, A.L. Willson had succeeded his father as secretary-treasurer of the York Township Council in 1866. Five years later he moved to Eglinton, buying a four-acre property at the present Sheldrake and Yonge. The price of $3,000 indicates that there was a good house on the property, but the Willsons apparently made considerable improvements.

Willson served the council until Henry Duncan was elected as reeve in 1880. The two men did not get along, and Willson's job was divided and given to two other men, William Jackes and John Knox Leslie (of Leslie Street). After running unsuccessfully against Duncan in the next election, Willson began the publication of a real estate paper. He continued to be active in local politics and was elected reeve of the township in 1888 and 1889.

The council was kept busy throughout the 1880s. The township area was reduced by creating a series of independent villages and municipalities. The council was not always unhappy to see them go. Most of the new municipalities were growing rapidly and had a variety of growing pains. From its beginnings in 1841 the council had maintained a conservative, rural point of view. In over 50 years there were only three clerks of council: John Willson, his son Arthur Willson, and William Jackes, son of Franklin Jackes, the first reeve.

For many years the area west of Yonge Street had dominated in council. William Tyrrell of Weston virtually reigned as reeve. In 1889 a new era began when Henry Duncan became reeve. Duncan's farm was on the northwest corner of Don Mills and York Mills. His fine red-brick Victorian house was a notable sight on that corner for many years, and as of 1990 was serving as a restaurant some 200 yards north of its original site. Duncan was a member of a powerful block of interrelated families — the Duncans, Mulhollands and Stewarts. He served as reeve for 22 years.

TORONTO ON THE MARCH

During the 1880s the Township of York lost a good deal of its territory. Six new villages were created, and five other localities were given directly to the city.

AREA	MADE A SEPARATE MUNICIPALITY	ANNEXED TO THE CITY
Parkdale	1878	1889
Brockton	1881	1884
Weston	1882	1954
Riverdale	*	1884
Rosedale	*	1887
Annex	*	1887
Seaton Village	*	1887
Junction	1887	1909
East Toronto	1887	1908
Sunnyside	*	1888
NORTH TORONTO	1889	1912

Incorporated directly into the city.

In the meantime some interesting people moved into the area. In 1877 John Strathy, a Toronto financier, bought 120 acres centred on the present Erskine Avenue. Two years later he bought the Harris farm at Glengrove East. If the first purchase was as an investment, the second was for a home. The Harris farm was much more an estate than a farm, a complex of buildings that had been built and carefully maintained by several generations of responsible and well-off owners — Jonathan Hale, Jesse Ketchum, and James and Fidelia Harris. It was renamed "Strathgowan," using Mrs. Strathy's maiden name of Gowan. Unfortunately, as is often the case, John Strathy had few years to live after he retired to this estate: he died only seven years after taking possession. One son, James, sold "Strathgowan" to Jesse Garland. Another son, Arthur, sold the Erskine Avenue property in 1886 at 100-percent profit!

Further north, Alfred St. Germain was buying up property. He was an interesting man, a direct descendant of Rudolph St. Germain, one of Jacques Cartier's lieutenants during his sixteenth-century voyages of exploration. He was born in Kingston in 1827 and became one of the proprietors of the Kingston *Herald*. He disappeared in California during the gold rush of 1849, turning up later in Toronto, where he published a newspaper, the first one-cent daily paper in Canada. On retiring, St. Germain began to buy up property on the west side of Yonge, in what is now Bedford Park. By 1883 he owned some 200 acres running north from the present Fairlawn Avenue. He ran his property as something of a gentleman's farm. (By the 1880s the term "gentleman" had taken on new connotations. In the early 1800s only those of "good family" and those wealthy enough not to work would have been called gentlemen. By the 1880s, if you were reasonably well off and "well and favourably known in the community," you could be called a gentleman.)

Visually, the area had changed very little over the years. Farm fields flanked Yonge Street from the cemetery hollow northward. There were only a few east-west dirt roads. Davisville ran east past the Cook farm and slaughterhouse that stood across from the present Davisville Park. The big trees that shorten the right field of the baseball diamond were the trees of the lane leading to the farmhouse. It was specified in the deed that these trees were to be left. Other Cook brothers farmed on two of the adjacent corners.

Davisville Avenue ran further east to link up with Bayview and the Lea farm (now present-day Leaside). Another short road ran east from the Davisville Pottery to the little ravine where the Davises obtained their clay. Eglinton Avenue — frozen, muddy or dusty — ran both east and west. Victoria Avenue ran out to Bayview and boasted a few homes and market gardens. Lawrence Avenue ran east and west through open farmland across the whole township.

The elms and maples bordering Yonge Street sheltered a wide variety of buildings, a few of brick but most of clapboard or rough vertical barn boards. In addition to at least three hotels, there were houses, barns, driving sheds, implement sheds, woodsheds, perhaps even icehouses — and certainly many outhouses!

Ice was cut during the winter with a special saw and was stored in blocks packed in sawdust. The writer recalls the block of ice at the pump, where the sawdust had to be

*In this picture of the "*PREVENTORIUM*" on Sheldrake Boulevard can be seen the pillars and cornices of the original private home belonging to Sarah and Arthur Willson in the 1880s. The house originally faced Yonge Street across a broad lawn. The house would later become the home of* EVANGELINE BOOTH *of the Salvation Army, and perhaps even a home for a ghost (see page 87).*

73

These pictures of the DAVISVILLE POTTERY *were taken about 1887 — some 60 years after the first pottery on the site.* ALEXANDER JOHN DAVIS *(far left) stands here with his employees and one lad too young to be a potter even in those days when child labour was not unknown. The building looks eminently practical, like most of the company's products. Somewhere in North Toronto there still may be examples of the green-glazed rose jars and jardinieres that were the pride of the pottery.*

carefully washed off. If you were about eight years old, and if the pump had a good head of water and a good leather valve, you could use all your strength on the downstroke and then be literally lifted in the air as the handle came back up. Samuel Hill, who farmed just north of Eglinton Avenue, east of Yonge, became the proprietor of the Ontario Ice Company.

Some of the farms, such as the Toronto Dairy Company and the Toronto Poultry and Produce Company, had now become specialized. Bryce's Dairy was growing steadily, and the dairy building would come to fill much of the area enclosed by the present Yonge, Lytton, Duplex and Craighurst.

The Davisville Pottery, however, was the oldest established business in the district. John Davis was a teacher or a bookkeeper who came to Canada from England in 1840. He learned the pottery-making business either at the Humberstone Pottery in Newtonbrook or from John Walmsley, whose pottery was on Yonge at the present Davisville until the 1840s. Perhaps Davis bought the pottery directly from Walmsley, because by 1845 it was known as the Davis Pottery, and John Walmsley died in 1846.

By 1870 there were six employees producing $4,000 worth of pottery a year, using clay from a small valley just east of Yonge. James Lesslie's diary complains that the local firms were not making good drainage tiles in the 1860s and that local farmers were dependent on imported tile. The Davis Pottery's main product was a very successful line of flowerpots and horticultural containers. The pottery continued to operate until 1932. During that time there were minor changes in the name and also in the location. It was moved to 377 Merton Street, and then further out to 601 Merton.

The Davis family was not content just to make pottery. John Davis was a very active man with a strong social conscience. It was not long before the area became known as "Davisville." Davis was the first postmaster, although the first post office was opened in Crown's grocery and feed store on the northwest corner of Yonge and Imperial. Davis also helped to build Davisville School and was a school trustee for 25 years. He was a founding member of the Davisville Methodist Church, which held its first service in a log building with a congregation of 25 people in 1851. By 1866 a new building was needed, and John Davis donated the land, just opposite Belsize Drive on Yonge Street. It was a frame building, to be rebuilt later as a red-brick church, which stood on Yonge until the 1960s.

Five Davis children survived to adulthood: Alexander, Frederick, Joseph, Francis and Sarah. All were active in the community, and most of them in the pottery. Joseph Stanley Davis became a justice of the peace. His first case concerned a casual labourer charged with drunkenness. Davis believed in firm measures: he gave the accused man five minutes to get out of town. If this judgment was given in the Town Hall, even the soberest of men would have had a hard time getting to the town boundary in the five minutes allotted! By the 1890s John's grandson "Jack" had built the Davis General Store (the building still stands on the northeast corner of Yonge and Davisville). In 1907 the *World* noted: "Jack Davis…as a storekeeper for groceries, flour and feed and fresh meat of all descriptions…he is hard to beat." Charles Davis, a grandson, had a good deal of success with his trotting horses. Joseph Stanley Davis was the mayor of North Toronto for 5 years and an active member of council for 13 years.

In 1885 Davisville and Eglinton were joined to Toronto by steel rails — well, not quite joined, but loosely connected. The Toronto Street Railway ran up Yonge to the foot of the hill below St. Clair. The new Metropolitan Railway started just below St. Clair and ran north to Glengrove. There was a short walk to get from one railway to the other. Both these lines ambled along at the speed chosen by the horses who pulled the cars. But this disjointed connection with downtown proved to be very popular. It was particularly useful for those senior students who commuted daily to the normal school or university, and for an increasingly large number of residents in the town having regular employment in the city. The coming of the electrified "radial" made possible the future of North Toronto as a dormitory suburb.

At the same time, C.D. Warren, acting for the Metropolitan, bought the north half of the Beaty farm at Glen Grove and established it as Glen Grove Park. It occupied roughly the space bounded by Glengrove, Glenview and Duplex avenues. For a few

The Pears house stood on the north side of Eglinton just west of the present Edith Drive. Behind the house the brickyard took up most of the valley floor almost to Roselawn; a little stream ran down the east side of the valley. Although the area is now Eglinton Park, all proper North Torontonians still refer to it as "Pears Park" (pronounced peers not pares).

years a Mr. King Dodds operated a race-track there, but it was not very successful. It then became a park used for lacrosse and baseball games, and a very popular place for picnics. On the Queen's birthday in 1892, the Toronto Street Railway loaned three cars to the Metropolitan to help them cope with the 4,000 people carried that day. The cars were manhandled with crowbars and wooden planks from one rail-end to the other!

In the same year that the Metropolitan came up Yonge, three significant men bought property in Eglinton.

James Pears was to give North Toronto its largest industry. He and his brother, Leonard, had come from England in 1851 and had engaged in brick-making with John Townsley. Their yard was on the west side of Yonge just opposite the present Rosedale subway station. By 1880 Pears had taken over the York and Carlton Brick Manufacturing Company, employing 60 men. But the area's clay was almost exhausted and the property was becoming valuable as Yorkville expanded northward.

Pears looked for a site for a new brickyard, and found it on Eglinton Avenue West, where Burke's Brook meandered south. There was a good supply of clay on the hillside — as the Indians had known 400 years earlier. Pears bought the property in 1885, and within a few years the *Recorder* reported: "Mr. James Pears, of Eglinton Avenue, will have a big season's brickmaking. He has fifty men employed this year and will burn about three million bricks, an increase of nearly half-a-million over the product of 1890."

The former Metcalfe estate at Bedford Park and Yonge as restored by PHILIP and WILLIAM ELLIS. The Metcalfes had moved back to Toronto after the house suffered a serious fire, but we can be sure that the Ellises moved in with executive vigour to restore the dignity of the house, gardens and stables.

Two colours of bricks were made, red one week and yellow-white the next. In the 1880s, two-colour brickwork was a popular feature of Ontario architecture, and one almost unique to Ontario. The Pears brickyard continued in business until 1926, when it was sold to the city as a park.

William H. Doel, like John Strathy, bought land in the Eglinton area as an investment and only later realized that it would be a good place to live. The investment was a farm on Bayview, now the site of Sunnybrook Hospital, but he bought property on Victoria Avenue as a site for his home. Members of the Jackes family occupied two corners of Victoria and Yonge. Doel's property was just to the east of these lots. Here he built a large and terribly solid-looking house. It stood well back on the south side of Blythwood until the 1960s. Its size can be envisioned by the fact that it was used as 12 apartments in the 1930s.

Doel was a prosperous Toronto druggist, but with a very interesting background. His father had been a brewer who was in sympathy with William Lyon Mackenzie and the

Reformers in the 1820s. John Doel's brewery served as a radical meeting place. Nevertheless, Doel withdrew his support as soon as Mackenzie announced his plan to use force. W.H. Doel, the son, became interested in history and was an active member of the York Pioneers, a historical society formed in 1869. One of his early acts in Eglinton was to join Thomas W. Anderson and Charles Durand — both of whom lived on Glengrove Avenue — in a campaign to raise a fitting memorial to Lount and Matthews, who were hanged in 1838. The remains of these two men were moved from Potter's Field to the Necropolis in 1859. Charles Durand claimed that he carried one of Lount's teeth on his watch chain from that time on.

There is a touching story about William Doel. His father had originally migrated to Philadelphia from England and, while there, had married a Miss Huntley before coming to Toronto. Many years later, his son, William, in turn, went to Philadelphia and found another Miss Huntley for *his* bride. One could hardly give one's mother a greater compliment!

Doel soon became a justice of the peace and was active in the North Toronto village council for a number of years. He died in 1905.

William G. Ellis and his brother, Phillip, were the sons of a civil engineer who was involved in railway construction. The brothers established a jewellery business in Toronto that became highly successful, eventually merging into the firm of Birks-Ellis-Ryrie (known for many years as simply Ryrie's to North Torontonians, and only later reluctantly conceded to be Birks).

The Ellises bought the old Metcalfe estate north of Lawrence at Bedford Park Avenue. The house and gardens were completely restored, but perhaps the most important elements of the estate were the horses and stables. These were important not only to Ellis, but to the entire community. High-quality horses carried more cachet in those days than do a Rolls Royce or a Lamborghini today. A high-stepper like Ellis's "Prince" was well known for its escapades. On one occasion, coming down Yonge Street, Prince bolted and threw his driver out onto the road, leaving little Reggie Ellis alone in the wagon and hanging on for dear life. The runaway veered onto Eglinton Avenue and into the cul-de-sac of the Salvation Army prison gatehouse yard, throwing Reggie out of the wagon, shaken but unhurt. (For many years the Salvation Army operated a halfway house on Eglinton Avenue, where their North Toronto citadel stands today.)

The Ellis brothers had plans for the development of the rest of the property. They envisaged a model village with local industrial employers and small homes with gardens for the employees. Fifteen hundred small lots were laid out (on what is now Bedford Park and Woburn avenues), but the Town Council refused to allow the industry. The

In the early years of the century even the humblest houses had a wooden picket fence. Few, if any, could match the magnificent gates and fences that fronted the Ellis estate. It is said that they were imported from England by Metcalfe, the previous owner.

77

A store had been established on the northwest corner of Lawrence and Yonge streets as early as 1846. It was operated by JOHN RUSSELL and then by his son JAMES. In 1885 it was taken over by JOHN ATKINSON (shown here), whose wife often looked after the store while he worked on the John Lawrence farm.

Ellises simply laid out Bedford Park and Woburn avenues, and waited for the prosperity to make them attractive.

William Ellis continued to live at "Knockaloe" until his death in 1929. His brother Phillip moved to a city apartment to accommodate his heavy responsibilities. He was a man who merited fame, but who neither wanted nor received it. Despite his own successful private enterprise, he was a strong supporter of public ownership of utilities. (The story of his part in the founding of Ontario Hydro and the Niagara Parks Commission is too involved to include here.) He was a commissioner of the Toronto Hydro Electric Commission from its founding in 1911 until his death. He was also a founding commissioner of the Toronto Transportation Commission from its inception in 1920 until his death. Throughout that time he was active and progressive. What is still one of the world's great transit systems seems to have taken much of its character from Phillip Ellis. In his epitaph, *Saturday Night* commented: "Few as were his public utterances, his name is written large over the history of an amazing transition period."

Good times returned in the late 1880s. It was with hope — and perhaps a little greed — that a number of areas were opened up for development: Sherwood and Keewatin (then Woodward) avenues; Castlefield and Roselawn (then Kensington) avenues; Briar

Hill and St. Clements (then Hawthorne) avenues; Craighurst (then Roper) and Albertus avenues; Sheldrake (then Crescent Avenue) Boulevard and Stibbard (then Franklin) Avenue.

But what is now North Toronto remained in three quite distinct parts. Davisville was separated from Eglinton by the Clergy Reserves (at Manor Road). Eglinton was separated from Bedford Park by the Lawrence and Anderson farms south of Lawrence.

Lots, however, were reasonably priced. A lot on Davisville Avenue, for example, could be bought for $300 — $10 down and $3 a month free of interest. Development was in the air, and people even talked about incorporation. The prerequisites for incorporation as a village at that time included a population of at least 750 in close proximity, and a petition of 150 resident householders and freeholders. These conditions could be met by combining Eglinton and Davisville.

On November 22, 1889, under By-Law 551, York County Council granted incorporation to the village of North Toronto. Four months later North Toronto was promoted to the heady status of an incorporated town.

A way of life was ending. Even the farms that remained were locked into a suburban setting. There were nearby shops for food and clothing, and even jewellery. The radial ran almost by the door. The farmer knew that his lands were irreversibly changing from farm fields to real estate. •

Sometimes it was very easy to "open up" a road. A horse and plough could be used to make furrows showing the edges of the 16-foot-wide road-to-be. Then, with horses and scoop-shovels, the topsoil would be removed. The centre of the road was left a little higher than the edges. When trees, rocks, streams, or steep grades were encountered, the task was much more difficult. Only when the roadway had been inspected and pronounced as "stumped, graded, and bridged" would the local Council assume the road and thereafter be responsible for its maintenance.

NORTH TORONTO
BECOMES A VILLAGE

The Council of the brand-new Village of North Toronto probably had its first meeting in this house on Yonge just south of Keewatin. The building served many purposes over the years, including acting as the local YMCA. It still stands, behind a welter of alterations.

O N THE DAY of incorporation as a village, the new council met in the YMCA Hall. The reeve was John R. Miller; the three councillors were Frank Langrill, George Robson and Joseph S. Davis. Their first act was to create a Board of Health and Sanitary Inspection, with Dr. George Jackes as head of the board. To be frank, the outhouse or "night-soil" situation had become a problem, both to the citizens' olfactory senses and to their health, as a direct cause of diphtheria. Septic tanks were effective, but uncommon. The so-called dry-toilet, which needed to be removed periodically, was the most common, and the "honey-dipper's wagon" moved in smelly silence through the community after dark. There were even "night-soil wars," in which one municipality would dump its collection onto an adjacent municipality. One pictures two such wagons with their redolent cargoes passing in opposite directions in the dead of night. The North Toronto Council and Dr. Jackes took prompt action to improve the situation.

The council had time for little else in the short life of the village. Four months later, on April 7, 1890, North Toronto was incorporated as a town. A new council took over the former York Township Hall, which became the North Toronto Town Hall.

The owners of the Metropolitan Railway now wanted to open their line up to the top of the hill at York Mills, and they wanted $15,000 from the township to help. The *Recorder*, a local paper, objected. The only reason the Metropolitan wanted to do this, they pointed out sourly, "was the booming of lots north of Glengrove Park...on the assumption that fools are born every hour, and suckers are plentiful most seasons." Undeterred, the radial built to the top of the hill, and then electrified and improved the line and the cars. (It was electrified two years before any part of the Toronto city system.)

Another railway project was soon to follow. In 1889 the Belt Line Steam Railway Company was authorized to build a line that circled through a number of Toronto suburbs. Within two years 90 men were working east of Yonge and 125 west of Yonge; the bridge crossing Yonge at Merton was almost finished. By 1892 steam whistles announced the coming and going of the Belt Line trains across the southern border of North Toronto.

The Belt Line had a dramatic copywriter who announced: "It will be a new era. It

This is 129 Blythwood Road in 1892. The house is clearly recognizable today, minus the picket fence. Built in 1885-86, as of 1992 it was occupied by James Ramsay's great-grandson and family. The house is listed with the Toronto Historical Board.

Eglinton School on Erskine Avenue, shown here after additions made in the early 1890s. Some parts of this structure can still be seen in the present John Fisher School; they are visible only from the east side.

will lift toiling man and woman for at least a little while out of the grime and scent and smoke of the city. A cheap fare, a comfortable seat, a well-heated, well-ventilated and well-lighted car, a quick ride, and here, on the Highlands...here the balmy air and zestful surroundings will win back bloom to the cheek and courage to the heart."

Unfortunately, not enough toiling men and women rode to and from the Highlands. Within two years the Belt Line Railway was bankrupt. Stations like the one at Yonge and Merton, and another at Eglinton and Chaplin, fell into disuse. For many years the Grand Trunk Railway, and later the Canadian National, used the track to supply businesses on Merton Street and at the north end of Lawton Boulevard. Today the bridge over Yonge Street still stands; the right of way west of Yonge has become a jogging track and walkway; and a very short section of the original track comes down out of the valley to cross the Bayview Extension just west of the old Don Valley Brickworks.

Although the Belt Line Railway was a failure, the Town of North Toronto was growing rapidly. In 1890 the town held 1,000 people; by 1910 it would grow to five times that size! The Town Council had much work ahead of it. Once they had the town smelling a little sweeter, they turned to other important projects, of which schools had become perhaps the most important. Nearly one-half of the town's people were children of school age. Years earlier it had been argued that not much formal education was needed if you were going to stay on the farm, but not many children in North Toronto would be staying on the farm. Schooling was becoming important.

By the 1890s there were two main schools, Eglinton School on Erskine Avenue and Davisville School on Millwood Road. The "old school" at Yonge and St. Clements had been moved back from Yonge Street and was no longer used as a school. It became known as the Orange Hall. There was still a one-room school at the southeast corner of Glencairn and Bathurst, but it was a county school. There had been another on the northeast corner of Eglinton and Bayview, but it had gone by 1892.

It was decided to make additions to both Eglinton and Davisville schools. Two contracts were awarded, to Fisher and Ramsay for Eglinton School and to William J. Hill for Davisville. It was fortunate that there were two contracts, because John Fisher was the incoming mayor and William Hill was the incoming reeve of the township.

The firm of Fisher and Ramsay had established itself firmly in North Toronto by building the Eglinton School, the Town Hall, and many homes in the area. John Fisher had married Elizabeth Snyder, but they had married late and had no children. Perhaps that was why he had the time to be active in local politics. The Fisher house was on Yonge just north of Broadway, and it is likely that an adjoining yard and outbuildings provided space for construction equipment and materials.

John Fisher became the first mayor of North Toronto; he had, in all, 11 years of service as mayor. Between terms, he served on the township and county councils. He was a man much respected in the district. When he died in 1911 he was honoured by the City of Toronto, the Town of North Toronto, and many, many friends and associates.

James Ramsay, Fisher's partner, had also married a Snyder, Rachel, and there can be little doubt that these marriages melded the Fishers and the Ramsays firmly into the community. The Ramsays raised a family that was interested in "every phase of the life in the new town of North Toronto." In a house still standing at 129 Blythwood, the Ramsays raised four boys: William, Harry (known as Dick), James and Roy. The two oldest boys were in the town band, which gave street concerts and was always ready to add life to a picnic or a fair. Dick Ramsay had a horse, a beautiful gelding called Valda, known, of course, to everyone in North Toronto. Not only did Dick and Valda win races at the Glengrove course, but also much further afield, at places like Markham and Aurora. Roy Ramsay was assistant coach and secretary of a very successful North Toronto hockey team. Several members of the family belonged to the volunteer fire brigade.

William J. Hill, the other successful bidder, was the third generation of that name in the area. His grandfather had bought the 200 acres on the southwest corner of Yonge and Lawrence in 1807, and had lived and died there. His father had been a carpenter and builder. We know of one of his houses on Yonge near Blythwood and others at the corner of Eglinton and Bayview. The third William Hill married a daughter of Joseph Bloor, whose brewery was in the valley east of Yonge at Yorkville. The Hills lived on Farnham Avenue in Deer Park. His company had good contracts with the Toronto Street Railway, laying the cedar blocks in which the car tracks of the time were embedded. He was active in city and county politics, and served as reeve of the Township of York from 1894 to 1897.

JOHN FISHER was a popular figure in North Toronto, a long-term mayor, and a partner in the construction firm of Fisher and Ramsay.

Mayor Fisher hardly needed to advertise for re-election. When he was not acting as mayor he was active on the councils of York Township and the County of York.

At the turn of the century there were a number of interesting families in the town. About 1895 John J. Gartshore had a large house built on the old Lesslie estate. You may recall that James Lesslie, prominent Toronto reformer and businessman, had bought the old Montgomery home in 1855. He and his wife, Jacqueline, retired there and called the house "The Willows." As they grew older, the 27-acre estate began to prove a heavy burden. Fortunately, John Gartshore, a cousin of Jacqueline, came to live with them and operate the farm. Lesslie died in 1885 and Jacqueline a few years later. The estate and the considerable Lesslie fortune were left to John Gartshore.

As a newly wealthy man, Gartshore found "The Willows" a little too old and, as it turned out, a little too small to house comfortably the eight Gartshore children. About 1890 he had a new, larger house built on the slope just to the south of "The Willows." He named it "Willowbank," and it still stands at the corner of Oriole Parkway and Burnaby Boulevard. The "old house" was used as a residence for visiting or retired missionaries, since Gartshore was deeply involved in the support of missions. But the whole family moved back into the "old house" briefly when the acetylene furnace in the new house blew up and made redecorating mandatory. The original Montgomery house was pulled down about 1910.

Most houses would still have had outdoor plumbing; lighting would have been kerosene lamps; and heating and cooking would have been by wood stove. A few of the newer and more expensive homes would have had heating systems and even indoor plumbing. One such house was Thomas Dack's home on Yonge just north of the present

"WILLOWBANK" was built to the south of "The Willows." From its windows, one looked over farm fields to where Upper Canada College was being built, and beyond to where Toronto church spires could be seen.

In 1837 John Montgomery's wife and childern may have watched from this verandah as Montgomery was taken off to receive the death sentence as a traitor. The house would later become "THE WILLOWS," the Victorian home of James and Jacqueline Lesslie.

Teddington Park Avenue, surrounded by a spacious lawn fronting on Yonge Street. As the years passed — and as the house passed into other hands — the property on Yonge was sold for a row of stores and for two large duplexes behind them. Yet there was still enough lawn for a gracious residence fronting on Teddington Park when the Stollerys of Yonge and Bloor fame lived there in the 1930s.

On the southeast corner of what is now Teddington Park, another older house faced onto Yonge Street. Called "The Cedars," it was a handsome and rather elaborate house, together with suitable stabling. The house, which still stands at 17 Teddington Park, was the home of the Pinder family. The former front lawn on Yonge now holds a bank and several stores, but the house has been turned 90 degrees so that it faces onto Teddington Park. It has been carefully renovated, but the original house can easily be detected.

Back in 1837 a "young Stibbert" was one of the men roped together and marched down Yonge Street as traitors; he was jailed and then released for lack of evidence. This was, we believe, Robert Stibbard Sr., a long-term resident of Eglinton. Although he had been a patternmaker in England, he became a market gardener in Eglinton. He settled on 20 acres of the Ketchum property almost out to Bayview. A right of way from Yonge was part of the deal, and this right of way later became Victoria Avenue, and later still, Blythwood Road.

Stibbard married a Miss Sheldrake. They had two sons and one daughter (who married into the Grainger family of florists). One son, Robert Jr., took over the farm on his father's death. The other, John Sheldrake Stibbard, bought some 40 acres in the area of the present Sheldrake and Stibbard. His farmhouse and barns very likely stood where Eglinton United Church now stands. The orchards ran eastward, and there are still original trees in gardens on Sheldrake Boulevard.

In 1887, infected by the subdivision bug, John Sheldrake Stibbard laid out Crescent Avenue (Sheldrake) and Franklin Avenue (Stibbard). He took down his barns and built a new house at the end of Crescent Road, overlooking the ravine. It became 394 Sheldrake and still stands in 1992. Behind the house, and used as a henhouse, was the body of an old horse-drawn coach which had been used many years earlier on Yonge as "Stibbard's Bus." For many years one of the original 1885 Metropolitan Railway cars rested in a valley behind the house. It was 16 feet long. The short street now known as Dalewood, which ran in front of the house, was called Beulah Avenue until at least the late 1920s.

John Stibbard needed patience as a land developer. A few people bought lots on his streets, but few, if any, houses were built in the next ten years. Finally, in 1904, Stibbard built a large duplex at Sheldrake in an effort to lure other builders. William Ramsay was one of the first to build. His house still stands on the southeast corner of Sheldrake and Dalewood; his son lived there until 1992.

The 1890s were not good times for the economy, but North Toronto continued to grow. As the schools improved, other social facilities tried to keep up. The number of churches was increasing. For some 50 years the Methodist Church at Glengrove East had been the only church in Eglinton. It had drawn many who were not Methodists, but who found it the only nearby church. Gradually, however, as more people arrived, little

JOHN SHELDRAKE STIBBARD, after whom two North Toronto streets are named. Robert Stibbard, his brother, had two daughters, Ethel and Lena, shown below on either side of "Miss Campbell." One of the girls married a Mr. Devereaux. Her father built them a home on the northwest corner of Sheldrake and Mt. Pleasant at the cost of $200! Painted dark brown, it was known as the "Chocolate Drop," and though remodelled it still stands today.

W. WALLACE JUDD as a corporal in the Boy's Brigade, dressed to the teeth and ready for the grand parade down in Toronto. The Brigade was a popular organization run by the Reverend Tibbs of the Presbyterian Church.

groups of other denominations began to come together. By 1890 St. John's Anglican, York Mills, had established a mission church in Eglinton. Services were held in the old schoolhouse until the little red-brick St. Clements was built. For a few years the first rector, the Rev. T.W. Powell, had driven down each Sunday from York Mills accompanied by Miss Emma Osler, who conducted the Sunday School. But by 1900 the vicarage had been built on the muddy lane that would later become Duplex Avenue. Zion Baptist Church was built on the northwest corner of Castlefield and Yonge. It would later be moved to Castlefield Avenue near Duplex. St. Monica's Catholic Church was built on Broadway with the financial assistance and encouragement of Eugene O'Keefe, a prominent Torontonian. For years Davisville had a small Methodist Church, and by 1900 a new, larger church in two-coloured brick was built on Yonge Street opposite the present Belsize Drive. Prime Minister Lester Pearson's father served as a minister at this church for a short tenure. Presbyterians met every second Sunday in the old schoolhouse. Deer Park Presbyterian was also popular with Presbyterians until such time as Eglinton Presbyterian was built at the northwest corner of Yonge and St. Clements.

In the 1890s there was a welling up of energy and time for sports and other local entertainment. This is recorded in two fine sources of the time. The *Observer* recorded the news of North Toronto on a weekly basis in the early 1890s, and Canon W.W. Judd's *Reminiscences* of the turn of the century is a delightful record, delivered as a talk many years later. Both these sources look at North Toronto through rose-coloured glasses, but the reader will realize that North Toronto also had its poor, its sick, its unhappy at the time.

Glengrove Avenue West circa 1900. The field at the right was called Glengrove Park. Horse races, annual fairs, and lacrosse games took place here, sometimes with literally thousands of visitors coming by radial to see the events.

A light-hearted view of life comes through in the pages of the *Recorder*: "The Alpha Tennis Club did not play last Saturday on account of *la pluie*...On Friday evening, a large party of residents in the town having regular employment in the city who were going home by the 6:30 p.m. car, got tired of waiting for connection (below St. Clair) and footed it home. The following morning, the same party, which included several young ladies, objected to paying fare, not having had the ride which they had paid the previous night. The conductor, failing to collect his fare...undertook to bounce the crowd with the assistance of the motorman. Loney Brown, who was about to be the first victim yanked out, began feeling the muscles of his arms and wondering whether they would stand him in as good stead as those of his legs which won him the gold watch at the Glen Grove Park Exhibition, when an old gentleman with a stout stick told the conductor he would knock him down if he laid a hand upon the guileless youth. That settled it, and we are informed all hands enjoyed a free ride to the city...The Citizens' band will perform a choice programme of selections on Saturday evening, weather permitting, at the corner of Broadway and Yonge...Sam Lawrence's horse ran away again yesterday afternoon, and made a fine smash-up of the rig...The lacrosse match between the newly-formed clubs of Eglinton and Deer Park took place at the Glen Grove Park yesterday evening in the presence of a large number of spectators, including ever so many pretty girls roosting gracefully on the fence."

The Stibbard house and the delightful ravine behind it were frequently the scenes of local picnics. One Queen's Birthday, the big 24th of May celebration, the Stibbards held a basket picnic for about 80 friends and neighbours in their "grove." "The provisions were very choice and abundant, being served out about six p.m. to people whose appetites were keenly invigorated by the woodland air, as well the hearty indulgence in football and baseball sports, several of the ladies present proving themselves to be old timers at the latter game.... In the evening, most of the party repaired to the fine new residence of Mr. Stibbard, where an impromptu programme of songs and instrumental music...did much to make the pleasure of everyone complete." On another, similar occasion a large basket was used to ferry guests high over the stream on a line stretched across from tree to tree.

It was a time of joining, of belonging to organizations, whether they were choirs, bicycle or tennis clubs, or the many more serious organizations, including the Orange Order, Masonic lodges, Knights of St. Andrew, Knights of Columbus and Sons of England for the men. For boys, there was the Eglinton Cadet Templars of Temperance. There was a Women's Institute. The YMCA, under its long-time local president John J. Gartshore, was apparently a co-educational organization; at least in its early days, women members outnumbered men.

It is astonishing that there are no public photographs of Glen Grove Park on a busy occasion, for the park was a centre of sports and social events. The Township of York had a Fall Fair that was held in Markham one year, Thornhill the next, and so on. When it was Eglinton's turn, Glen Grove was crowded with people watching horse races, lacrosse games, and doing their own judging of exhibits, from heifers to pumpkin pies.

Have we a ghost story here?
GENERAL EVANGELINE BOOTH of the Salvation Army lived in the big old Willson house at the corner of Sheldrake and Yonge. Many years later, writing to her friend the Hon. Herbert A. Bruce, Miss Booth wrote: "During my early days in Canada when you came up to save my life at the ghost-haunted house in Eglinton...." Perhaps this was humour, but for those who pursue the occult, this letter is quoted in Dr. Bruce's autobiography.

At Glengrove and what is now Heather Avenue, a private drive led off to ANSLEY CASTLE, or "Beaver Hall," which stood at the top of the low hill just east of the present John Ross Robertson School. The "castle" had been built for Alfred Ansley, a successful manufacturer of men's hats — and hats were de rigueur *in those days. It is said that the very handsome house at 76 Glenview was built for his son Marcus Ansley, and that a similar house stood just down Glenview; it was removed when Duplex was put through. It is also said that Mrs. Ansley fell on hard times when her husband died. There are touching stories of her visits to the neighbours with a pail when the castle's water was cut off. More readily verified is the fact that pieces of the concrete castle were used by neighbours for rockeries when it was demolished in 1925. The above picture shows the estate in dire need of a gardener.*

Glengrove Avenue West was bordered on both sides by tall pines, and a brick sidewalk ran up the south side of the street. The park was on the north side, running from Yonge to about Ansley Avenue. Four private homes stood on the south side. One was owned by John Anderson, who still owned most of the land now occupied by Chatsworth, Cheritan and Chudleigh avenues. Another house stood at the present corner of Glengrove Avenue and Heather Street; it was occupied by a Mr. Charles Frogley, who ran a bakeshop in Yorkville. (As of 1991 the bakeshop building still stood at the southwest corner of Yorkville and Yonge.) A third house was on the southwest corner of the present Duplex Avenue. Well-known today as "Leptis Magna," it is one of the oldest and largest houses on Glengrove, with 27 rooms.

At the other end of town from Glen Grove was the cricket pitch at Davisville. The Town Council supported athletic clubs, even to the extent of giving them small annual sums of money. This sometimes created strange situations. In 1920 the Davisville Yonge Men's Club asked the council for more money because the Eglinton Yonge Men's Club had badly used the Davisville field, presumably damaging the cricket pitch. The council, in turn, threatened to cut off funds from the Eglinton Club for the damage. The Eglinton Club resisted. Over a period of time the whole matter sank to rest and nature repaired the cricket pitch. The council continued to support sports: for example, the Bedford Park Skating Rink received free water and two free electric lights.

Running races were held on Yonge Street on holiday occasions. In the 1890s bicycling became almost a craze. The old "penny-farthing" bicycles, with one small and one large wheel, had made cycling a very difficult feat. Now the "safety bicycle" had become the "in" thing. The main attraction was the freedom that cycling offered. Girls could appear modern and independent in stylish clothes that exposed their ankles, while retaining grudging social approval. The bicycle craze affected Yonge Street, of course. A newspaper reported that "among the good results that will follow, the watering of Yonge Street will be that it is sure to become a favourite route for the holiday trips of the bicycle clubs. The Toronto Bicycle Club went as far as the Green Bush, Steeles Avenue, on Saturday week, and are loud in their praises of the table set by Mr. Steele." Another admirer of Yonge Street was "Mr. J.W. [John Wycliffe] Forster, artist…who intends to take his class sketching at Bedford Park."

Yonge Street was becoming too busy. On taking over, the Toronto City Council reported that "at present, this section of Yonge Street is…most dangerous owing to the congestion of Traffic and street car service." The radial had reached as far as Jackson's

Point on Lake Simcoe by 1907. Weekend trips to Lake Simcoe became enormously popular with Torontonians, and day trips with a picnic to Bond Lake, just south of Aurora, attracted thousands more.

Radial traffic increased phenomenally. Passenger traffic grew from 350,000 in 1900 to 2,240,000 in 1905! There were even regular railway freight cars in use on Yonge Street, sometimes up to 100 cars a day. At Bond Lake the radial connected with a steam railway running 14 miles to Schomberg. Down Yonge Street came carloads of milk, and carloads of ice from Simcoe Lake. For many years the radial had the greatest volume of any inter-city electric railroad in Canada, despite the fact that no trains ran on Sundays until 1910. (Between 1895 and 1897 the trains were allowed to run on Sundays, but only to carry milk to the city.)

The crowding of Yonge Street caused the Town Council to create a "Parallel Roads Committee" with a mandate to provide alternate north-south streets through the town. Duplex Avenue came into being as a result of "duplexing" Yonge Street. With only one legal case to delay it, the new road was put through from Imperial Avenue right up to the Fox Creek ravine north of Glenview Avenue, but it was a good many years before that ravine was filled in and

This electric coach, built in 1907, and was a passenger car complete with smoker and lavatory — and stained-glass windows.

Picnickers at Bond Lake just south of Aurora. The clothing indicates a date of approximately 1910. The radial cars, which would wait to take the picnickers back to town, were heavy-duty interurbans capable of speeds of well over 60 miles an hour.

Duplex could continue northward unimpeded.

Redpath Avenue was also considered as an alternate north-south road, but someone built houses on the north side of Keewatin, so Redpath went no further. Mt. Pleasant Road took a lot of planning and bargaining. The township had to give approval to drive the road through Mount Pleasant Cemetery. In the end it was agreed that the cemetery would be given the old Belt Line right of way through the cemetery in return for what became Mt. Pleasant Road. As it was built northward, Mt. Pleasant passed through the De Ferrari property at Broadway and then through the edge of the Ussher property at Blythwood. But just as Duplex came to a halt at the Fox Creek ravine, so also did Mt. Pleasant. The stub end of Mt. Pleasant ran down north of Blythwood Road to a sandy end among the pines at the ravine's edge, until the bridge was built in 1934.

In 1909 the planned subdivision was introduced to North Toronto. The Dovercourt Land, Building, and Savings Company had just bought the Lawrence farm at Lawrence and Yonge. They brought a new concept in planning and set out to build fairly costly houses in a tasteful environment. Lots were 50 by 150 feet and cost from $15 to $75 a foot, depending on location.

The financial mind behind Lawrence Park Estates was Wilfred Servington Dinnick, son of an Anglican minister, and a man of culture, as well as an aggressive financier. He was active in charitable affairs, and he threw himself into vigorous action on the outbreak of the Great War, becoming Lieutenant-Colonel of the 109th Regiment that sent some 5,000 men to France. He was active in the British Red Cross, and in the Toronto and York Patriotic Fund. He organized and promoted backyard garden contests in Toronto, with awards and prizes for those who made the best use of their home gardens.

The home of W.S. DINNICK, ESQ., the financier who began building the Lawrence Park Estates around 1911.

The estate was laid out by Walter S. Brooke, a British engineer. His concept was to take advantage of the area's natural landscape and offer a complete contrast to the gridiron pattern that had been the basis for most planned communities since the days of Rome. Adaptive planning was being received with enthusiasm in England. Hills were not levelled, nor were major trees cut down. Houses and gardens were planned to harmonize with their surroundings. Many of the gardens were well landscaped and had terraces, croquet lawns and gazebos. The principal architects were Chadwick and Beckett, who carefully adhered to the standards set out by the Dovercourt company. The first six of these houses were completed by the outbreak of World War I in 1914.

Lots in "The Park" received tasteful promotion. But there were many areas in Toronto for people with this kind of money — Moore Park, Lower Forest Hill, etc. This competition, and the restrictions caused by the war, slowed sales. Dinnick was hard pressed and resigned as president of the Dovercourt Land, Building, and Savings Company.

Like most of North Toronto, Lawrence Park was built starting at Yonge Street and only slowly filled in further back. The author recalls Lawrence Park in the 1920s and '30s. Dawlish and St. Leonards were built up to just a little past St. Ives. St. Ives itself

This house, 181 Dawlish Avenue, was built for Magistrate JAMES EDMUND JONES in 1914 and originally stood on a much larger lot than it has today.

had a sprinkling of houses, but Rochester, Cheltenham and Buckingham did not exist. The whole of what is now Lawrence Park east of St. Ives was scrub land, not the fair farm field described by Canon Judd in 1900, but fields that had gone to waste over a period of years, mostly overgrown with hawthorn bushes. It was a paradise for boys — ideal for dug-in forts and mock battles. A future music publisher, a senior airline pilot, and a doctor specializing in the physiology of weightlessness were all killed many times in these mock battles. In the meantime Dinnick and his brother — the latter with the grand name of Augustus George Cuthbert Dinnick — had got in even deeper by spending $500,000 for the land which had been the Clergy Reserves. This property was still in rolling farmland and ran from the present Manor Road to Belsize Drive. In a letter dated 1911, Augustus Dinnick wrote: "It is the intention of my people to develop this property along strictly high-class lines, and while not perhaps exactly as the Lawrence Park Estates has been developed, you may take this as a guide to what we intend to do."

Walter Booke laid out the new area, avoiding again the strictly rectangular, and winding his roads around the hillside, where the Church of the Transfiguration has never quite been able to take full advantage of a superb site. The houses of Glebe Manor turned out to be modestly priced, a reflection of the demand that did not arise until after World War I.

These developments were just part of the great changes taking place in North Toronto at the time — a great influx of people and a changing lifestyle.

The change of lifestyle is a little harder to trace. Perhaps something of the transition comes across in the Bedford Park picture. Taken about 1910, the board-and-batten wag-

The growth of population is easy to trace:

	1890	1912	1921	1925
c.	1,000	6,000	13,000	22,000

	1930	1935	1948
	45,000	69,000	70,000

on works is flanked by the Bedford Park Hotel. Between the two, and attached to the wagon works, is a frame house whose verandah can just be seen. A present-day relative recalled the simple lives of the couple who lived in this house. Much of the life in the old village can be summed up in the statement, "They were poor, but they didn't know it."

Piped water was coming to North Toronto, but both the house and the hotel would still get their water from a pump, probably an outdoor pump. The hotel had been built with metal eavestroughs, but the older house would almost certainly have been built originally with board troughs to catch the rain and run it into the rain barrel. Most early houses had a rain barrel, since the soft water that it collected was the best water for washing ladies' hair.

Behind the house and hotel would have been vegetable gardens, small orchards, and probably a henhouse. (The North Toronto Poultry Association was a very popular organization at the time. Annual meetings had to be held downtown in order to find a hall that was spacious enough.) There were myriad flies and sometimes other unexpected visitors. One resident remembered, "One day, my grandfather came home with a large picture that he had bought for the sake of the frame, but when he removed the picture from it, he discovered the inside was alive with bedbugs."

The pump was often dangerously close to the privy. Much of the food was produced

THE BEDFORD PARK WAGON WORKS with the Bedford Park Hotel at the right and a small farm house in between. These buildings were on this west side of Yonge just immediately south of Fairlawn Avenue.

and kept in less-than-sanitary conditions. Milk, for example, was not pasteurized until 1914. Refrigeration was only a box with a block of ice. By today's standards, people led lives of constant peril from bacteria, if not poison.

Cooking and heating was made possible by wood-burning stoves. Woodsheds were the norm, and maintaining a supply of firewood was one of the duties of the man of the house. A good provider kept his wife supplied with wood that had been at least one full year under shelter to dry. Not any wood would do: the best firewood was maple or beech; elm sputtered and crackled too much; pine and other softwoods burned too fast (although they made good kindling). Good baking was a matter of judgment, and the quality of wood for the stove was as important as, and much more demanding than, the controls of today's stoves.

By 1910 some furnaces were being built into North Toronto homes, and the domestic use of coal was becoming common. Mr. Bristow of Leaside exemplified the change. He had started by selling firewood which he got by breaking up old freight cars from the CPR shops at Leaside, then he progressed to selling kerosene when kerosene heaters had a brief run. Finally he ended up selling household coal in 1915. Elias Rogers, of course, lived royally in Deer Park on the sale of coal, and by 1915 sales in the north end of the city justified the establishment of a branch coal yard at the north end of Lawton Avenue.

A view of Weybourne Crescent between St. Edmunds Drive and Dawlish Avenue. The future site of Alexander Muir Memorial Gardens is in the foreground — more tastefully landscaped today.

Medical assistance was available to north-enders, but with few if any of the life-saving drugs that would become available in the near future. Pneumonia could easily prove fatal; consumption, that terrible wasting disease, was just being brought under control; to have diabetes was to have a sentence of death. Almost one-half of the people who entered hospital in 1910 would die there.

There were, however, four medical doctors in Eglinton in 1905: Dr. Bond was at Roehampton and Yonge; Dr. Doherty on the west side, opposite; Dr. Jeffs was on Yonge, across from Glencairn; and Dr. Richardson was "somewhere on Yonge Street." But for many people of that time, doctors were a matter of last resort except in cases of childbirth or a serious wound. There were hospitals, but only in downtown Toronto. Dr. Campbell Meyer's hospital in Deer Park was a sanitarium rather than a hospital as we know it today.

In 1909 the Town Council authorized the opening of a high school. It consisted of two classes meeting upstairs in the Town Hall and separated by a very thin partition. George "Shorty" Reed was the principal, and for a year or two the school devised its own curriculum — after two years it bent enough to accept the authority of the Ontario Department of Education. In 1910 the council authorized the sum of $28,000 for the construction of a building, and on December 7, 1912, the cornerstone of North Toronto Collegiate Institute was laid.

For most people, social activity centred around the church. In 1975 Charles Basset Brown, nephew of the last mayor of North Toronto, recalled: "The Church of today cannot possibly be the Church of my parents, who knew, personally as a friend, everyone who attended, and to whom the Church was the centre of their lives, not only for religion, but for recreation and fellowship...." The churches offered many services and related organizations. There were two services on Sunday, plus Sunday School in the afternoon, plus a prayer meeting in midweek. Or one could join in Missionary Aid Societies, Ladies' Aid Societies, Young People's League, Epworth League, Boys' Brigade, Mission Band, Women's Missionary Auxiliary or other similar groups. And of course there were church dinners and Sunday School picnics.

North Toronto's first church, EGLINTON METHODIST, built in 1834 on the southeast corner of Glengrove Avenue and Yonge. Originally called "the brick church," it was later stuccoed to hide the scars of a serious fire. By 1922, when this picture was taken, the drive shed for horses had been removed and a number of small additions had been made — presumably without benefit of an architect. However, the congregation made up for this by building the award-winning Eglinton United Church on Sheldrake Boulevard. The Toronto Hydro substation replaced the old church.

Regular church attendance for the very young could prove very boring, but while the sermon was being delivered, there was time to be observant, as Brown recalled: "...the organist I think was Miss Florrie McCormack...the organ was a small pipe organ which was pumped by hand by a handle in the rear. A small string with a red weight would show the pressure. If the pumper dozed and the pressure went down, the organ would let out a squeak and the music stopped. This naturally startled the organist, as well as the pumper, who would frantically renew his efforts at the pump. Later, we got a wonderful pipe organ which was worked by water power, as we still had no electricity, with the exception of the large carbon lights at each corner on Yonge Street.

"The long sermons were almost unbearable for a child, and for some older people too, and I remember looking out the Church windows and seeing people I knew walking home from the Anglican, Baptist and Presbyterian churches in the Castlefield-Yonge district and wondering why our service kept on and on and on.

"If any work or play was indulged in on Sunday (I wasn't even allowed to ride my tricycle), the person was soon told how wrong this was...Even the small lending library in the Sunday School had a motto over the door saying the only payment required for the loan of a book was a request that you refrain from the use of tobacco and all alcoholic beverages."

In the years just prior to North Toronto being annexed to the city, the mayor was Alonzo Brown, a Davisville jeweller. May Brown's father was William "Irish" Brown, who had come to Eglinton in 1870 and for 40 years had been the township and village assessor and tax collector. He and his wife, Louisa (Danbrook), had eight sons. One,

Edwin, operated a store in Eglinton; another, Frederick, went west as member of the Royal Canadian Northwest Mounted Police and married an Indian girl; a third, George, moved to Chippewa and drove the trolley that ran along the edge of the Niagara gorge.

Alonzo, the youngest brother, and in 1911 the mayor of North Toronto, lived on the west side of Yonge, three houses south of Eglinton, and later moved to 99 Alexandra Boulevard. He married Cecilia Ward of Eglinton. Alonzo was a very active joiner, Master of York, Deputy Grand Master of the Grand Lodge of Canada, a Potentate of the Ancient Arabic Order of Nobles of the Mystic Shrine, Provincial Grand Prior of the Knights Templar of Canada, a member of the Oddfellows, the Foresters, and the York Pioneers, as well as councillor, reeve and mayor.

In a corner of the Town Hall, near the front door, was a small raised area, around which curtains would be drawn for privacy. The mayor and council met, usually in the evenings, in this corner. There were also less formal meetings. Across the street, just south of Erskine Avenue, there was a euchre club on the second floor over a store. The movers and shakers of North Toronto got together there informally.

Mayor Brown and his five councillors proved to be an astute group, dealing quickly with some matters, while delaying others for the city to handle later. By 1911 the mayor and the council had successfully postponed the sewage question by the accepted political expedient of calling for a long series of technical reports. The matter of the town water supply was nursed along. There was sufficient water for the present. In 1900 the town bought property in what is now Sherwood Park. Artesian wells flowed freely there, the water was pure, and a pumping station had been built. (Some of the heavy piping remains on the steep hillside immediately west of the present Works Department building.) Only the future could determine whether the supply of water could keep up with the demand, so the matter was left for the future.

The town had been seriously studying the relative merits of gas and electricity. Both systems had already reached North Toronto. Electric streetlights on Yonge Street, generated by steam power on Roselawn Avenue, had proven to be popular. But gas had been brought up from the city as far as Eglinton, and some people were connected to it. Houses were built on Sheldrake Boulevard, with gas pipes for lighting, even before the gas lines came that far north. By 1911 the decision was made in favour of electricity, and the town sought tenders. Three quotations were received: from the Toronto Electric Light Company, the Interurban Electric Company, and the Toronto Hydro Electric System. This was an unusual case of direct bidding between two private companies and one publicly owned company. The decision was made in favour of Toronto Hydro,

The Town of North Toronto pumping station in Sherwood Park supplied the town with water from artesian wells nearby. It stood — minus the tall chimney — until the late 1980s. There are unconfirmed reports that local natural gas was used to fire the boilers.

NORTH TORONTO IS ANNEXED BY TORONTO IN 1912

MAYOR ALONZO BROWN
decided to make much of the situation:

*Whereas the installation of the Electric
Lighting system for the streets and houses
will be completed by July 1st, next: [1911]
And whereas the event is noteworthy in
the wonderful progress and development of
the town: Therefore, be it resolved that the
Council request that Dominion Day be set
apart by the Citizens for the celebration of
the turning on of the Electric power to
light our streets and houses: and that the
Fire Brigade, Town Band, the High
School and Public Schools, the Churches,
Lodges, and other oganizations of the town
be invited to cooperate with businessmen,
real estate operators, and citizens
generally on assisting the Council to make
the celebration a success.*

North Toronto Council, *Minutes* 1911

THE DAY CAME, THE SWITCH WAS
THROWN, THE ELECTRIC LIGHTS CAME ON.

perhaps because the city was constantly battling with the private companies, or perhaps because P.W. Ellis was head of the Hydro system.

Annexation to the City of Toronto soon overshadowed all local problems. The town was becoming a dormitory suburb, and the citizens clamoured for improved transport to replace the aging radial. In 1911 newspapers were regularly commenting on the three-sided debate between the town, the city, and the Metropolitan Railway Company. No agreement was reached. Nevertheless, annexation was becoming inevitable, and a local plebiscite was held in June 1912. The *Globe* reported that the "the June plebiscite resulted in a close victory for annexation — 604 to 543 — although only Davisville showed a majority in favour. Eglinton was perhaps jealous of local autonomy, and Bedford Park was too concerned with the transport issue."

In 1912 City of Toronto By-law 1195 authorized the annexation of North Toronto to the City of Toronto. The Town of North Toronto simply became Ward 9 of the city. •

Yonge Street looking south from Roselawn Avenue in 1917. Two radials pass one another while heavily-laden sleighs carry hay to the stables of downtown Toronto. The Acme Hardware at the left stayed in business there until well into the 1950s.

Bedford Park in 1922

*Verandahs and fruit trees, the radial, and a team
of Clydesdales, but across Yonge Street, the stylish
stone gates that marked the opening of Wanless
Avenue to construction. In the centre of the picture
can be glimpsed the store that still stands at the
northeast corner of Ranleigh and Yonge.*

THE
TOWN OF NORTH TORONTO

BEFORE BECOMING A TOWN, the Village of North Toronto extended from Mount Pleasant Cemetery to just north of Blythwood Road, and ran 1,000 feet east and west of Yonge Street. After incorporation, the town limits were extended north to Glen Echo, and the eastern and western town limits followed the rather strange pattern shown in the map **T-1**. This still remained the boundary of the city as of 1990.

The two maps make an interesting contrast, one drawn up in 1892 for the *Recorder* newspaper, **T-1**, and the other being the first official topographic map produced in 1909 for the Department of Militia and Defence. **T-2**. The 1892 map is ahead of its time, showing a number of roads that existed only on the plans of developers. The 1909 map, on the other hand, has been unable to keep up with the extremely rapid development that took place in the years after 1906. Nevertheless, the three divisions of the town are clear: Davisville, the most populous; Eglinton, beginning to sprawl out east and west; and Bedford Park with the sparse beginnings of subdivisions.

By 1905 Davisville consisted of about 200 buildings, and new construction was continuous on Davisville, Balloil and Merton avenues. Merton and Balliol were presumably named after two colleges of Oxford University. Unfortunately, Balliol was misspelled with two L's, and the original pronunciation was lost. It became Buh-LOIL to a generation of streetcar conductors and thus to most of the people of North Toronto. Building, however, was confined largely to a few streets. There were still roads, like those shown in **T-3**, that were bordered by farm fields, especially in the Glebe area between Belsize and Manor Road. The future Chaplin Estates were simply part of the fields extending up to Eglinton west of Yonge.

Davisville included the south side of Eglinton Avenue. The centre of activity, however, was at the corner of Yonge and Davisville. On the southeast corner was Lemon's Hotel, with the Skinner house just south of it. The southwest corner was probably taken up by George Plumb's greenhouses. The northeast corner was the store of Jack Davis, **T-4**, with the

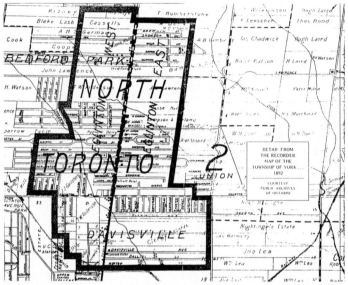

T-1. Detail from the 1892 recorder map of the Township of York.

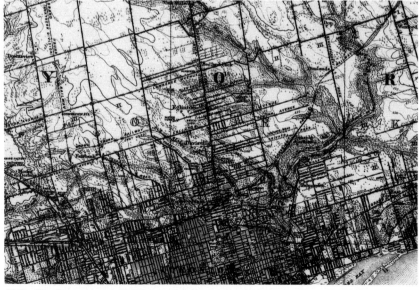

T-2. The Department of Militia and Defence topographic map drawn in 1909.

T-3. *A rural road in Davisville, 1906, when there was more green and less noise.*

T-4. *The Davis General Store, built in the 1890s by Jack Davis.*

T-5. *Looking north on Yonge Street from Davisville.*

T-6. Fording the Don River on Eglinton Avenue East.

T-7. Mr. G.E. Coon's grocery at the northwest corner of Yonge and Eglinton.

T-8. *Looking south from Broadway and Yonge.*
T-9. *Looking north from Broadway and Yonge towards the Town Hall.*

Davis Pottery a little north of that. On the northeast corner of Millwood and Yonge stood the home of Joseph S. Davis, who served as magistrate and also mayor of the town for one term. Just east of Yonge was the enlarged Davisville Public School. (J.C. Rutherford was the principal, assisted by two other teachers.) Proceeding north, **T-5**, there were homes, some of them quite old, on both sides of Yonge. They were fronted, for the most part, by picket fences and a screen of trees. On one side or the other of Yonge were the harness maker, a jeweller, a blacksmith, a butcher and a lumber yard. The Methodist Church stood on the west side of Yonge opposite the present Belsize Drive. In 1905 Davisville had 41 buildings on the west side of Yonge and 27 on the east side. There were 41 buildings listed on Merton, 34 on Balloil, and 24 on Davisville.

Small market gardens and old houses occupied the southwest corner of Yonge and Eglinton. The Moore estate was prominent on the east side of Yonge just north of the present Soudan Avenue (see page 53); the estate was complete with spacious lawns and good stabling. (The *Recorder* noted that almost an entire streetcar was taken up by the Moore family and baggage when they set off for their summers in Muskoka.) Westward on Eglinton there was open farmland as far as the present Oriole Parkway; the homes of the Bales and the Bescobys stood further up the hillside. To the east of Yonge was the Salvation Army Prison Gate House, a halfway house that gave ex-prisoners a chance to fit back into society. It also operated a bakery that became popular in the district. Eastward beyond that was the Toronto Produce and Poultry Company. Short roads led south off Eglinton, and a few scattered houses were built on these streets.

The north side of Eglinton Avenue was part of Eglinton. Mr. Coon's store, **T-7**, was a place where men would sit around a wood stove in cold weather. People collected at this corner; the gentleman with the straw hat and umbrella is a classic model of the time. Coon was known to give candy, and even bananas, to children. Perhaps this paid off, because he is said to have won the Irish Sweepstakes and retired.

Westward on the north side of Eglinton there was a livery stable, a few small houses, and then the Pears Brickyard. Further up the hill stood the Gartshore estate, with the old house, "The Willows," standing to the north of the new house, "Willowbank." Further west, Eglinton Avenue, still a dirt road, rambled off through farm fields to the hamlet of Fairbanks at Dufferin Street. East of Yonge there were 23 scattered dwellings on the north side of Eglinton. The Don was crossed by means of a ford, **T-6**. South of the road as it entered the valley was a clay pit that helped supply the Davisville Pottery. The village of Eglinton, while not as populous, was a little more impressive than Davisville — probably because it boasted the Town Hall and Oulcott's Hotel, **T-8** and **T-9**, on either side of Montgomery Avenue. Across Yonge from the hotel was the handsome fence and screen of trees, **T-10**, behind which stood the Maguire house, while across from the Town Hall was the residence of John Fisher, who served several terms as mayor. North Toronto homes at that time were usually built close to Yonge Street, but there were still open spaces and fields close to Yonge. A cow could graze comfortably behind the Town Hall, **T-12**. (The wooden shed behind the Town Hall was the temporary firehall!) Roselawn Avenue — at that time called Kensington — was one of the few streets that ran an appreciable distance from Yonge. Lawrence's greenhouses, **T-13**, "headquarters for all that is beautiful in floriculture," was on the north side of Kensington at the present Rosewell. Up the hill and past today's Avenue Road stood the standpipe from which the Town of North Toronto obtained its water pressure. The location was, and is, the highest point in the City of Toronto. Water had been obtained from the nearby hillside, but by 1902 new sources were needed. Large circular wells were sunk in the ravine at the end of Sherwood Avenue to tap the artesian wells that flowed out of the ground there, and a new pumping station was just able to keep up with the demands of a fast-growing town.

Eglinton also had a solid business area, **T-11**, **T-14**, from just south of Erskine to just north of Sherwood Avenue. The Eglinton portion of North Toronto was also home to three churches; the Hygienic Dairy (between Lytton and Craighurst); one new and one retired schoolhouse; and a somewhat run-down "Castlefield," beyond which houses were being built on a street of the same name. There was also the sizable home of Evangeline Booth, daughter of the founder of the Salvation Army.

As Yonge Street reached the hill at Lawrence Park, farm lands took over on both sides, although the Lawrence Park subdivision was becoming evident by 1912. Bigger and older homes were set well back from Yonge — "Strathgowan" (the old Ketchum-Strathy house), Franklin Lawrence's house atop Lawrence Park Hill, and Thomas Anderson's home near the corner of Chatsworth and Yonge. Fields continued on both sides past Lawrence Avenue, **T-16**, and up to Bedford Park Avenue. There was a little cluster of activity at the Atkinson store, **T-17** and **T-18**, and the Ellis estate of "Knockaloe." Further north, on the west side, was the Bedford Park Hotel and some 20 other buildings. On the east side there were only

T-10. The entrance to the Maguire home at the southeast corner of Broadway and Yonge.

T-11. The shopping section on Yonge north of Erskine in 1910.

T-12. *Behind the Town Hall (left) and Oulcott's Hotel (right). The small building above the cow was the temporary fire hall.*

T-13. *The Kensington (Roselawn) Avenue greenhouses owned by Councillor W.J. Lawrence.*

T-14. It must be either March or December as we look north on Yonge from Keewatin.

T-15. A view of Castlefield Avenue taken about 1909.

T-16. Looking north on pastoral Yonge Street (near Glengrove Avenue) in 1898.

six buildings north of Lawrence. Finally, two large homes stood on either side of what is now Yonge and Teddington Park (see pages 84 and 85).

Even as late as 1912 the Town of North Toronto was essentially Yonge Street, with little fingers of streets reaching out into fields. •

T-17 & 18. John Atkinson's store on the southwest corner of Bedford Park Avenue and Yonge was a commercial centre in the 1920s. The change from buying in bulk to packaged goods was in full swing, but the refrigerator, with chests above for blocks of ice, was not quite ready for frozen foods. The scale on the counter was made in Toronto by International Business Machines, a name adopted by an American company when it took over a small Montreal company that was using the name.

THE
PEOPLE
OF
NORTH
TORONTO

A snapshot from the 1920s.

P-1. THE JUDD FAMILY lived on Blythwood Road where Blythwood Road Baptist Church now stands. The picture was taken on July 3, 1897. Elizabeth Judd, recently widowed, brought her family to Victoria Avenue to be near two of her married daughters. Mrs. Judd is in the centre of the picture with three of her unmarried daughters grouped behind her.

On the lawn at the left, with his dog, is William Wallace Judd, the youngest son. After the picture was taken he would probably have gone across the road to pick up his good friend Roy Ramsay, and together they would have taken off into the valleys and woods that characterized rural Eglinton. Eighty years later, the same man, now the Reverend Canon W. Wallace Judd, after a full life for his church, would still visit shut-in members of St. Leonard's Anglican Church and leave everyone feeling better for his visit.

Cannon Judd's reminiscences were given as a talk in 1972 and give us the best and most human description of North Toronto at the turn of the century. He had the remarkable ability to keep in touch with his North Toronto childhood friends, finding them in Winnipeg, in Nova Scotia (where he was headmaster of King's College School) and even in the far west. In his eighties, he frequently found time to sit at the bedside of his old childhood friend Roy Ramsay.

P-2. This is a full family portrait of the De Ferrari family of North Toronto taken soon after 1900. The older gentle-

P-1. THE JUDD FAMILY

P-2. *The De Ferrari Family*

P-3. *The Waddington Family*

P-4. *Mossie May Waddington, Aileen Dewdney and Valerie Dell Waddington*

man in the centre of the picture appears to be the patriarch of this nuclear family. Most of the males are wearing ties, and one is looking handsome in a uniform, perhaps that of the North Toronto Band. The one woman, handsomely dressed for the occasion, proudly displays the youngest child. The young girl at left centre is beautifully dressed and carries a small bouquet; can this be a confirmation dress? Surely the one woman did not cook, wash, and keep house for all those men!

The De Ferrari family operated a market garden on the north side of Broadway Avenue. The house was just west of, and the lot included, land used for the future Mt. Pleasant Road. Behind the house the land slopes down to a small stream that made its way roughly down Broadway to the corner of Eglinton and Bayview and thence to join the Don River. It was an excellent site for a market garden and orchard. Their success is evident: three horses and a skittish colt, as well as a delivery wagon and a family carriage. Don't forget the family dog — a smooth-haired terrier standing on the rump of the central horse. In 1911 Mt. Pleasant Road cut through the property. The family received $2,400 in payment, but they took their fruit trees, sold the remaining property, and moved away.

P-3. Next door to the Judds on Victoria Avenue was the home of Herbert Waddington, Mrs. Judd's son-in-law. The house still stands as 98 Blythwood and can be clearly recognized from this picture, which was taken in 1909. The picture shows Mrs. Waddington, her mother, Mrs. Judd, and five of the six Waddington children — Mossie May, Valerie Dell, Melville, Olive and Norval. The Waddingtons moved a few years later to a large home on the southeast corner of Heather Avenue and Glengrove, formerly the home of Charles Frogley.

Herbert Waddington was in real estate, in partnership with Fred Grundy, who built a spacious home well back from Yonge on the northwest corner of Albertus Avenue. Eventually, of course, stores were built on Yonge, in front of the house, and for a few years the Grundy house served as the YMCA, and during the Depression as three separate apartments. Sometime in the 1960s the house was taken down and replaced by the present numbers 14 – 22 Albertus Avenue.

P-4. Mossie May and Valerie Dell Waddington on either side of Aileen Dewdney at just about the turn of the cen-

P-5. MR. & MRS. ALFRED ST. GERMAINE *in their Still auto, 1898.*

P-6. MRS. BRENNAND *and the family cow.*

tury. One of these girls would become a Greek scholar, tennis star, mother, and Dean of St. Hilda's College.

P-5. Mr. and Mrs. Alfred St. Germaine in their Still auto of 1898. St. Germaine foresaw the future of the automobile. His car was quite probably the first Canadian-made car to reach the hands of a private buyer. "It weighed 750 lbs., was powered by a 5-horsepower air-cooled gasoline engine, and cost $750.00. The unusual-looking steering wheel not only steered the car, but, when pushed forward, it made the vehicle drive forward, and when pulled all the way back it engaged a reverse gear."

A Toronto group had formed the Still Motor Company that became the Canadian Motor Syndicate in 1897. The Syndicate produced one car that year and at least one more — St. Germaine's — in 1898, using British patents. At about the same time, the Lozier Manufacturing Company at Toronto Junction set out to manufacture bicycles, typewriters and automobiles under American patents. In 1899 it became Canada Cycle and Motor, with its car component named the Russell Motor Company. On the basis of present evidence, the Canadian Motor Syndicate may well have been the first into production (Canadian Motor Museum).

St. Germaine was very interested in the future of the automobile. An omnibus was to be built by the Canadian Motor Syndicate. It was to be used on The St. Germaine Pioneer Autocar Line, a line which does not seem to have gone beyond the planning stage.

P-7. CLARENCE BRENNAND and the Davisville Hockey Club about 1912.

P-6. The Brennand Family lived on the east side of Forman Avenue between Eglinton and Soudan avenues. In this picture, taken in 1909, Mrs. Brennand is milking the family cow. Her husband was the town assessor, and for that purpose had one of the first telephones to be installed in North Toronto.

P-7. Their son, Clarence, was active in the Davisville Hockey Club and is shown kneeling, front row right. He went on to become a fighter pilot in the Imperial Royal Flying Corps in World War I. On his return to North Toronto, he became a teacher at North Toronto Collegiate Institute.

P-8. Military matters were a source of pride in turn of the century North Toronto. Here is the militia, the 12th York Battalion of Infantry, at their annual camp near Niagara,

P-8. The 12th York Battalion of Infantry.

looking very warlike with triangular bayonets affixed to their Snider-Enfield rifles. The men wore scarlet tunics, dark blue pants with a red stripe, a dark forage cap, gleaming black boots, and dramatic "pipe-clay" crossbelts.

The Boer War broke out in 1899, but the stout Imperial hearts in the Toronto area were military-minded and ready. The first axes on Yonge Street had been those of soldiers. Most of the early settlers had been in the army, and many remained active in the militia: De Hoen was a captain in the Rangers; James Ruggles was an ensign. Men of the York Volunteers fought along side the Indians at the capture of Detroit. Later, on their way to Queenston Heights, the General had said, "Push on, the York Volunteers." The phrase was changed to "Push on, *brave* York Volunteers" and became a song well known to every North Toronto child well into the 1920s.

The 12th Battalion became the 12th Battalion of York Rangers, authorized to use the motto *Celer et Audax*, the motto of the first British regiment raised in North America. (It exists today as the Queen's York Rangers, with headquarters at Aurora, Ontario.)

North Torontonians relished the pomp and splendour of Queen Victoria's Jubilee in 1897 — the Bengal Lancers in brilliant turbans, Australians with cocked bush hats, Ghurkas with savage knives, Highlanders, African, Fijian and Newfoundland troops, as well as the splendid Royal Canadian Northwest Mounted Police. Looking back, we can see it as a build-up to World War I. At the time it was the pride of the Empire.

When the Boer War broke out, every man in the 12th Battalion volunteered.

P-9. Some happy snapshots from the 1920s. The picture at the top was taken at Pear's Park. We can identify the Bedford Parkers in the middle picture, from left to right: Gordon Atkinson, Miss Pearson, Miss Lena Rankin and Ralph Presgrave. How many tens of thousands of informal family portraits have been taken in North Toronto over the years? The bottom picture, courtesy of Flo Barrington, shows costumes of the '20s with Eglinton Avenue East as background.

P-10. John James Mackintosh, Chief of Police for North Toronto in 1911. He and his horse, Victor, were well-known and effective. He even found time to be a house-painter, since criminals found North Torontonians unsympathetic and alert. •

P-9. Snapshots from the 1920s.

P-15. *Chief of Police* JOHN JAMES MACKINTOSH *and Victor.*

THE CITY AND NORTH TORONTO

ADOPTION BY THE CITY did not affect many North Torontonians. They were busy building new houses and a new lifestyle. The Toronto City Council helped this process by taking quick action on some of the main concerns in the new ward. Sewers, water supply and paved roads were all approved, albeit without commitments as to when. These improvements gradually took place over the course of the next 25 years.

The new houses were very different from the old village ones. Not only did they provide for a furnace and central heating, but many were designed to have water supplied to a bathroom as well as a kitchen. After 1912 building seemed to follow the laying down of water mains. A minor peculiarity was that, while many of these earlier houses had kitchens, the sinks were put in very small adjacent rooms called the pantries.

Building lots came in many sizes and prices. Early in the century the most common price was $10 per foot of frontage, and suitable terms of payment could be arranged. In Bedford Park, Mr. Ellis's small lots could be had for 60 cents a week.

There were few restrictions as to the size or quality of the house to be built, and it was understood that there could be chicken coops or pigeon roosts at the back of the lot. Since the horse was still the main means of local transport, stables were as normal, if not as numerous, as garages are today.

This picture, taken in 1911, looks northeast from the present corner of Manor Road and Redpath, and shows frame houses and outdoor privies — the latter long since replaced.

The results of this unrestricted building can be seen on many North Toronto streets — adding a touch of variety pleasing to some people. There are still frame homes in North Toronto that predate the city by-law that insisted on houses being of masonry. There are also more recent masonry houses overlaid with siding to *look* like frame houses. Streets like St. Clements (to Rosewell), Hillsdale and Glengrove show a mix in styles and in years. Streets like Chatsworth and Chudleigh are examples of a more homogeneous style.

Frame houses and kerosene lighting created a need for good firefighting facilities. The Town of North Toronto had maintained three small outposts of the Volunteer Fire Brigade, and by 1910 fire alarms had been installed in the homes of some firemen. Old-timers recall, almost with awe, the daily fire practice — harnesses dropping from the ceiling onto the horses, the ringing of bells and pounding of hooves as the pumper swept out of the fire hall. It was a gripping sight, and if continued blasts of the Water Works steam whistle indicated that it was a real fire, the scene was one that could not be forgotten.

Fire Chief F.A. Murphy was a heroic figure to a generation of children. Murphy's status was so great that it reflected on his son, who was treated with near reverence in the schoolyard. Firefighters were paid $2 per fire; by 1916 Chief Murphy was compelled

Ankle-length oilskins, classy helmets and glossy horses distinguished these Bedford Park firefighters even before annexation by the city. Frame houses and wood stoves made the firefighting service an important one.

Joseph Kilgour's "Sunnybrook" when gardens and lawns were just beginning to spread out into the cornfields around the estate. The living room was hardly typical North Toronto! One looks in vain for a really comfortable chair, and woe to the maid whose job it was to polish the wood and dust the bric-a-brac.

to ask to have his salary of $100 a year doubled in order to stay ahead of his men.

In the same year that the Dinnicks began to subdivide the Lawrence farm into spacious 50-by-150-foot lots, Joseph Kilgour bought about 200 acres nearby, on which to build himself a home. It was the old Pabst property on the east side of Bayview — splendid open fields and wooded hillsides, with Stibbard's Creek and the Don River running through the bottomlands. He called the estate "Sunnybrook Farms."

Kilgour was a highly successful businessman whose paper bags and containers were widely used. His move into the countryside was the result of an urge to farm, and he wasted no time getting started. His big, rambling house was well back from Bayview south of Stibbard's Creek. Because the little bridge on Bayview just north of Eglinton was flooded by almost any rainstorm, the approach to "Sunnybrook" was from Eglinton Avenue on a drive which has become Sutherland Drive.

The barns, which still exist, show that Kilgour was serious about farming. As soon as his fields were in top shape, he arranged to host the York County Plowing Match, an event of tradition and importance. In 1913, 27 teams of horses competed in setting the finest and straightest furrows — with one tractor also entered. Today, of course, Kilgour's barns are at the centre of a huge recreational park; some barns are used as stables by the Metropolitan Police. The upland fields provide space for soccer and field-hockey fields, and for a number of cricket pitches. The Rothman's Annual Field Trials bring top-level equine attractions. Kilgour would have approved.

The Kilgours lived happily at Sunnybrook until 1929. They had no children, and when Kilgour died, Mrs. Kilgour left most of the property to the city as a park. It was Toronto's largest. During the thirties it was known officially as Kilgour Park and unofficially as Sunnybrook Park. A narrow paved road ran east from the entrance at the corner of Blythwood and Bayview, then wound down into the valley and alongside the Don for some distance. The southern part of the estate was sold and eventually came into the hands of the mysterious Captain Flanagan, and later into the hands of the Crown. That section is now the home of the Canadian Institute for the Blind and a number of other equally beneficial institutions.

Kilgour was astute as well as generous. The land was not just left to the government; any changes from a park required the consent of Kilgour's nieces or their descendants. That is why the decision to build the Sunnybrook Military Hospital in the 1940s required the approval of some very private people.

Up and down Yonge Street there were a number of large old homes that had originally faced Yonge but had sold their Yonge Street frontages for the building of shops or smaller homes. One of these was the old A.L. Willson homestead that had later been the home of Evangeline Booth of the Salvation Army. It now stood facing onto Sheldrake Boulevard, still with two or three acres of lawn.

This home was given to the Imperial Order of the Daughters of the Empire (IODE) in 1912 by Sir William Gooderham. This benevolent social order remodelled the house and operated it as a "Preventorium." It was a valuable and almost unique institution in the days when consumption was a prevalent wasting disease. The concept was not to take care of those with consumption, but to offer a healthy environment to other young members of afflicted families. The pictures make it obvious that it provided an active and healthy setting (see page 12).

Consumption was brought under control, and by the 1940s few children needed the protection of the Preventorium. The building became a convalescent hospital for members of the Royal Canadian Air Force; Air Force roundels or targets were emblazoned on the walls. After World War II the building was again used for needy children, but by the 1960s it had been pulled down and replaced by two streets of houses, Brynhurst and Georgian courts. The property under these names is still owned by the IODE.

A face to remember, and spirit to match, Dr. Emma Leila Skinner-Gordon was surely one of North Toronto's most admirable citizens. Raised as Emma Skinner, a farm girl on Yonge Street in Davisville, her life was marked by tenacity and love of others.

Born in 1859 or 1861 Miss Skinner had a normal farm upbringing. It was not until she was 35 years old that she became one of the first women physicians in Canada, graduating with an M.B. from the University of Toronto in 1896 and with an M.D.C.M. from University of Trinity College in 1900. After graduation Dr. Skinner specialized in obstetrics and gynaecology, and realizing the need for clinics for poor women in Toronto, she founded the city's first out-patient clinic for women, on Sackville Street. She was also instrumental in the opening of the Dispensary for Women and for many

Looking at this face, can you see the Davisville farm girl that accomplished so much?

years worked for its expansion. Together with Peter Rutherford, she organized the raising of funds for a 50-bed hospital at 125 Rusholme Road. By 1916 plans were made to expand the hospital to accommodate 160 more beds. Dr. Skinner was a very active fund-raiser.

Although not directly responsible for the present Women's College Hospital building, it is generally agreed that she was the inspiration behind it. She was in charge of the pediatric department of Women's College Hospital (W.C.H.) when it was at Rusholme Road, and she lectured on obstetrics for a number of years. As Dr. Skinner-Gordon, she was chief of the Department of Medicine of W.C.H. from 1910 to 1923.

In 1923 she established the Baraca Club, a religious and educational club for boys. Although these were boys with troublesome records, they willingly occupied themselves under her guidance. She was also the founder of the Merton Street Gospel Mission

Stalled in the mud, with a motor to start by cranking, what this poor man needs is certainly not an audience with hands in pockets, nor a passenger who seems full of advice. Yonge Street was just not ready for this 1913 Russel car.

in Davisville, and she was a campaigner for the Christian Temperance Union and a director of the Industrial Schools Association of Toronto. In 1908 Dr. Skinner married Henry B. Gordon, a Toronto architect and city councillor. She died on March 27, 1949, at about 90 years of age. Her husband outlived her by a few years. Dr. Skinner-Gordon made abundant use of her life in helping the less fortunate. A plaque dedicated to her has been erected in a small park on Merton Street.

When St. Germaine drove his early automobile past the run-down Bedford Park wagon works at the turn of the century, it might have been seen as a portent of things to come. St. Germaine was ahead of his time. The radial was still the life line of Yonge Street and would remain so for some years. Before automobiles or trucks could really be useful, the roads would need to be greatly improved. In 1909 the Bell Telephone Company bought a Tudhope car in Orillia and had it driven to London, Ontario, by way of Yonge Street, etc. It took three weeks to get there. It was 1923 before the first official road map of Ontario was produced.

In this postcard an entire class at Erskine Avenue Public School (now John Fisher) is knitting scarves for the troops in France.

The radial had reached the top of Hogg's Hollow by 1892 and Jackson's Point on Lake Simcoe in 1907. This was the beginning of a phenomenal growth in passenger traffic, from 350,000 in 1900, and 2.2 million in 1905, to a peak of nearly 10 million in 1921. For a whole generation of Torontonians, the most favoured summer trip was on the Metropolitan to Lake Simcoe. Almost as popular was a picnic at Bond Lake, just south of Aurora, where a steam launch called *Gypsy* would quietly puff its way around that little body of water.

In August 1914 World War I broke out. North Toronto, British to the core, accepted the war as the newspapers presented it, a war of self-defence against "the Hun." In the four hideous years that followed, 600,000 Canadians were sent overseas and 60,000 were killed. Because of their bravery at Ypres, the Canadians were treated as shock troops in the vicious slugging in the mud of northern France.

This is the Robert Inman family on the porch of their St. Clements Avenue home on the day before he left for France and "The Great War." He was killed in active service. Twenty-five years later the baby would be Lieutenant Robert E. Inman, one of the Canadian officers loaned to the British Army in World War II.

Torontonians and North Torontonians responded to the war with almost savage enthusiasm. A woman journalist wrote: "If you have not given a machine gun yet you had better hurry up…Everybody's doing it, doctors, lawyers, bankers, Daughters of the Empire. The Ministerial Association of Toronto, in solemn session, decided to give an extra good gun." Recruiting meetings were held in local theatres; streetcars carried enlistment banners.

In 1915 T.L. "Tommy" Church was elected mayor of Toronto and retained that office from until 1921. He proved to be the popular and responsive leader needed in the unhappy wartime years. No troop train left Toronto without his farewell salute, and he was always ready to help the families of overseas soldiers.

The home front was busy. Children in their classrooms knitted for the troops. Women's euchre clubs rolled bandages. Eaton's and Simpsons pooled their delivery services. Gasoline was rationed. "Heatless days" were declared. One February night, it was estimated that 3,000 tons of coal were saved — and 143,000 Torontonians went to the movies that night to take advantage of collective body heat.

The Great War brought two major social changes. The Temperance Movement had been active for many years, but now all alcohol was to be channelled into wartime industrial use. In 1916 the Ontario Temperance Act made alcohol very difficult to obtain. In 1921 an overwhelming vote made Ontario, to all official notice, completely "dry." There were, however, local boot-leggers, some of them driving taxicabs for quicker delivery. The number of doctors' prescriptions for brandy also increased. In 1927 legislation set up a provincial Liquor Commission and "local option" became a matter for each provincial riding. North Toronto voted "dry" and continued to do so until the 1960s. (The Jolly Miller at York Mills and the old Rosedale Hotel below St. Clair were the closest "wet" spots for 30 years.)

The World War I airfield at Armour Heights. The view is to the northwest. The present Highway 401 runs just about where the hangers stood. Fortunately more planes than airmen were racked up at the airfield by those daring young men.

More important than the temperance issue was the surge of interest in women's rights and responsibilities during the war. Mrs. Archibald Heustis, a North Toronto woman, was a leading figure in this movement. Available pictures show Mrs. Heustis as very much the "grande dame," posing with dignity in her home, "Birchknoll," at 1109 Mt. Pleasant Road. But much of her work was done as a young mother with four small children. She became president of the Women's Emergency Corps that undertook to register women who were willing to do men's work. Mrs. Nivin, Jesse Garland's granddaughter, recalls that one of the old houses on Yonge just north of Blythwood was used as a branch of the Women's Emergency Corps before reverting to its regular local charity duties.

A not very edifying situation arose. Many men found the good wages in wartime industry much preferable to the mud of France, and their unions solidly opposed "help" from women. Women, in response, began to favour the forced conscription of men into the army. In 1916 the Toronto Local Council of Women, another of Mrs. Heustis's organizations, voted in favour of conscription. One year later the federal Conservatives gave the vote to women in return for support in the touchy "conscription" election of 1917.

Meanwhile the Imperial Flying Corps set up aerodromes for training flyers at Leaside and Armour Heights, just northwest of the city limits. The combined airfields were called the North Toronto Flying Station. There were three squadrons at Armour Heights and two at Leaside. By 1917 some 200 flyers were training at Armour Heights, some 40 of them Americans, reported in the papers to be "almost all graduates of Yale or Harvard."

The people of North Toronto soon became used to the noise and excitement of these low-flying planes. Curtiss "Jennies" were used for training, and they were being built on Bathurst Street. A collection of photographs in the City of Toronto archives shows all too vividly the high percentage of crashes when daring young men first met flying machines. Amelia Earhart spent a good deal of time at the Armour Heights airfield when she visited her sister in 1917.

In 1918 Canada's first airmail shipment (Toronto to Montreal) took off from the Leaside airport. And in the 1920s Armour Heights was left as a rough field with the concrete foundations of hangars half-hidden in the grass, and perhaps a total of half a mile of paved runways. It was a great place for roller skating or for flying model airplanes. Down in a side valley of the Don were the machine-gun platforms and "butts" where the airmen practiced marksmanship. It was a spooky place for youngsters.

The Salvation Army had come to North Toronto quite early, just six years after its founding in London, England. It had built a "Half-way House" on Eglinton and had set up General Booth's daughter in a fine home on Yonge at Sheldrake. In 1912 the Salvation Army decided to build a training college in Davisville. Commissioner Rees spearheaded a successful drive to raise $100,000 — a great deal of money in those days. A site east of Yonge on the north side of Davisville was bought from Frederick Davis. The William Booth Memorial Training College building was completed in 1917. Of course the war intervened. The fine new building was generously turned over to the Military Hospitals Commission, which decided to make it into a Military Orthopedic Hospital. It was typical of the Salvation Army, which became well known for generous support of soldiers far from home. Eventually, the Salvation Army regained possession of its training college. As the picture shows, it was an imposing building in the Davisville of the mid-century, but it was demolished in 1962. A new college was built on Bayview Avenue, the present Isabel and Arthur Meighen Lodge for seniors was opened in Davisville in 1959, and the Salvation Army Retired Officers' Residence in 1965.

The war brought more traffic to Yonge Street. The airfields at Leaside and Armour Heights needed people, supplies and construction materials. The Leaside Munitions Company employed some 600 people. Although the railway ran a daily train from downtown, and although some houses for employees were built, a great many workers came up Yonge and across to Leaside by Merton Street or Soudan Avenue. James Bristow ran a bus service on various local routes. The fare was five cents. The Military Hospital at Davisville added to the traffic congestion.

Under this pressure, radial service began to sag and North Toronto tempers began to rise. By 1919 meetings of protest were being held in the old Town Hall. Withdrawal from the city was brought up at meetings filled with cries of "shame" and "coward." Mr.

The brand-new Salvation Army Training College was turned over to the government during World War II. It was used as an orthopedic hospital.

Aeroplanes were very popular. When Eaton's started the Santa Claus Parade in the 20s, it was decided to have Santa fly in from the North Pole. Accordingly, a plane landed him in a field near Yonge and Eglinton.

T.J. Pugh cried out that "the natural residential district of North Toronto had been blessed by God, and neglected and cursed by the City Council."

In the meantime the city council was wrangling with the owners of the Toronto Street Railway and its network of companies. Sir William Mackenzie's vast empire — Canadian Northern Railway, Toronto Railway Company, Electric Development Company, Brazilian Traction, etc. — left little time or interest for such small offshoots as the Toronto & York Radial Railway Company. To many Torontonians, it seemed obvious that "the making of substantial profits was the sole objective of the private owners of public transportation services in Toronto…They gave in quality and service to the public only as much as they could be forced to give under the terms of their franchise contracts." These contracts were due to expire in 1921.

In 1921 the new Toronto Transportation Commission took over the street railways of Toronto and the North York radial. One of their first acts was to promise to run regular Toronto streetcars right up to the city limits on new double trackage. R.L. Baker, president of the North Toronto Ratepayers Association, admitted that it was "the first thing they had

Yonge Street looking north to Lawrence Avenue in October 1922. The City of Toronto had taken over the old Metropolitan Railway and the new double streetcar tracks were in place. It was that interesting time when horse-drawn wagons were as common as automoblies. The concrete-laying machine was driven by steam, while the ditcher in the foreground seems to be gasoline powered. There were still four sets of poles, as well as an occasional streetlight. The picket fence on the left would mark the old Anderson home just north of the present Chatsworth Drive.

done for North Toronto since annexation." Actually, the concept of municipal ownership was becoming very popular since the publicly owned Hydro-Electric Commission was proving to be efficient, popular and cheap. The success of the TTC, and of the Hydro, owed much to P.W. Ellis, who was chairman of both these huge enterprises and brother to Bedford Park's W.P. Ellis. His view of the job was simple: "I am not a politician or a lobbyist. I am a business man. And I will not serve the Hydro or any other system, except upon the basis indicated." He remained in this dual commissionership until his death in 1929 — an excellent servant of the public in the best sense of the phrase.

In 1922 regular Toronto streetcars reached the city limits. For the first time, North Torontonians could feel they were really a part of the city. No more little hick railway; no more walking to change trains below St. Clair; no more extra fare. It had taken ten years, but the results justified the wait.

Yonge Street was properly paved, with double streetcar tracks running up the middle of the road. Within two years of taking over, the TTC had 575 big, new steel cars in operation, and a huge new terminal was nearing completion on Yonge just below Eglinton. It was an unaware soul who did not admire that great complex of tracks and the handsome administration building designed by North Toronto architect Murray Brown. Some of the tracks still remain in the bus garage under Canada Square.

The 1920s were high times, remembered fondly by most of the people who lived them. Somehow those hundreds of thousands of soldiers came back from France and

most of them found some kind of work, and somehow there began to be money for modern conveniences and little extras.

Prices had risen during the war — costs of groceries and consumer goods had risen alarmingly. The Toronto Police Commission reported that food prices were giving distributors from 200-percent to 1400-percent profit! It was that active North Toronto woman Mrs. Archibald Huestis who led the attack against the profiteers. She formed a group called the Producers' and Consumers' League, and with help from the IODE, she pressured the Attorney General of Ontario into charging the Wholesale Grocers' Association with price fixing. It was virtually impossible, of course, to find such an important association guilty, but some of the testimony was eye-opening. The William Davies Company, a huge Toronto meat packer and part of the Sir Joseph Flavelle empire, had shown an annual profit greater than its invested capital, and this in wartime while its president was being knighted for service to Canada. Apples bought from the farmer at 70 cents a barrel were sold by wholesalers at $5.25! Publicity had its effect. No one was found guilty, but prices quickly dropped to prewar levels. Even the federal government got into the act: the income tax, small as it was then, was reduced a little. In the twenties and thirties a single man earning $1,500 a year (a good wage) would pay only $18 in federal income tax. In 1926 it was possible for a husband and wife with four children to own a home and car, and get by on $25 a week. Unfortunately, most Canadian workers did not make that much.

Building took off again after the war. New subdivisions seemed to be of a higher quality than many of the earlier ones. Teddington Park, the Chaplin Estates, Alexandra

A new streetcar terminal opened in 1922 at the city limits, close to where the Yonge Street toll gate had stood in earlier times. It was here that one transferred from the city system to the radials running north as far as Lake Simcoe. This line was operated for a few years by Ontario Hydro. Traffic declined rapidly in the 20s. It was cut back to Richmond Hill in 1930, and in 1948 the entire service was shut down in favour of buses.

A large service and garage building for the radials was erected in 1922 behind the terminal, but as radial service declined, this building and space became successively a North Toronto Farmers' Market, an automobile dealership, and a supermarket. (The picture shows two weight scales offering "honest weight" for one cent. These were larger copper cents, and no one called them "pennies.")

(continued on page 124)   121

The laying of the consecration stone in the south wall of ST. CLEMENT'S ANGLICAN CHURCH *in April 1925.*

The Churches
of North Toronto

IN THE 1920s and 30s, the visitor would have been surprised by the number of churches in North Toronto. This almost uniformly Anglo-Saxon community worshipped God through many creeds.

In the early 1920s, Anglicans, Methodists and Presbyterians predominated. St. Clement's built a fine new church on the old site and helped to establish Anglican "mission churches" such as St. Leonard's. (St. Clement's itself had its origin as a mission church of St. James, York Mills.) In the mid-1920s, Church union became an important issue for Methodists, Presbyterians and related faiths. The majority of each of these congregations voted to join the new United Church of Canada. A few minorities went their own way. Out of the little Presbyterian church still standing at St. Clements and Yonge emerged two new handsome churches, St. George's United and Glenview Presbyterian.

The MERTON STREET GOSPEL MISSION in 1937, located on the south side of Merton east of Mt. Pleasant Road. Dr. Emma Skinner, pioneering woman physician, was deeply involved with this mission.

ST. LEONARD'S CHURCH was moved on rollers across the fields from Bowood Avenue to its present site on Wanless Avenue. In the early 1920s the men of the congregation faithfully moved the church a few yards every Saturday.

Meanwhile other churches were springing up. Roman Catholics outgrew their little St. Monica's and built the splendid Blessed Sacrament on Yonge Street opposite Lawrence Park. There were many smaller churches, like the Merton Street Gospel Mission. Sometimes church-going was a "hands-on" activity. Warren David recalls the early Bedford Park Methodist (Fairlawn United): "What has really stuck in my mind was the building of the white frame church.... I remember Dad dashing home from work, having supper and [going] over to the church with the other men of the congregation and literally building the church. Dad was a carpenter and the rest of the trades were well represented in our congregation." (While this church was being built, the congregation met in the old Bedford Park Hotel, where the minister used the hotel bar as a pulpit. Of course, with prohibition in effect, the bar had long since dried out.)

St. Leonard's was originally built on Bowood Avenue, but a new site was purchased on Wanless, close to Yonge. Men of the congregation put the church on beams and rollers, and Saturday after Saturday, they dragged and pushed the church across the fields to its new location.

Churches were still the centres of social life. Most North Torontonians, if not active churchgoers, still adhered to one church or another. Easter was an important and solemn occasion with great hymns, followed by a very secular visit to the Sunnyside boardwalk in the afternoon. Christmas Sunday brought everyone out. The pageants at almost every church peopled North Toronto with an astonishing number of angels and shepherds. •

Church pageants were regular social events.

The new Yonge streetcars were very impressive. This picture looks forward past the conductor on the right, with the stove opposite, to the front of the car, where the motorman was semi-enclosed so that he could concentrate on the traffic.

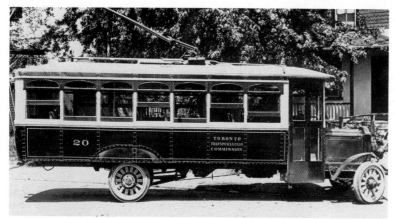

Canada's first trolley bus went into operation in 1922 on the Mt. Pleasant route. In this picture it is backing out of the laneway used as a "wye," preparatory to heading east on Merton to Mt. Pleasant. Note the hard rubber tires.

Park and Lawrence Park West became popular with the almost upper-middle class. A distinctive feature of nearly all of these houses was a front porch or verandah, sometimes quite a spacious porch. Today visitors from Britain and Europe often comment on this feature. Until the early twenties, few houses were built with a garage, as it was expected that public transport would take care of that sort of thing. Inside the house was not only a bathroom, but a tiled bathroom, using the little six-sided white tiles about the size of a modern dollar coin. Some houses even had more than one bathroom! All had coal-fired furnaces, and a coal bin in one corner of the basement. Wooden planks confined the coal, but not the dust caused when the red-and-black-faced coalman carried sack after sack of coal on his back and dumped them through a basement window. (As a boy, I wondered why my mother would spray the incoming coal with the hose. I worried about whether the wet coal would burn; it never occurred to me that it was to keep down the dust.)

In each house one person had the responsibility of "keeping the furnace in" — that is to say, not to let it go out at four o'clock in the morning and yet not letting it consume too much coal. This was a matter of experience and judgment. The only thermostat was the temperature of your skin. Coal came in many sizes and qualities. Anthracite, or hard coal, from Pennsylvania was used for heating most North Toronto homes. The best and hardest was "cannel" coal for use in fireplaces. Furnaces and stoves burned other hard coal in sizes favoured by the user.

The average house in North Toronto could be kept fairly comfortable for about $100 per year. Few houses used fuel oil, and as late as 1922 city council had to approve each application for an oil fuel tank. Insulation was almost unknown, although old newspapers were sometimes wadded in to fill open spaces around the windows or under the eaves.

The housewife — and there were very nearly as many as there were houses — was not encouraged to leave the house. Almost every kind of food and service came to the door in the 1920s and 30s. Eaton's and Simpsons each delivered twice a day every weekday. Simpsons' wagons were pulled by grey horses; Eaton's by bays (dark brown with black mane and tail). This service meant two trips a day from Queen Street up to North Toronto and back, with lunch taken down at Queen while reloading for the afternoon delivery.

Bread wagons, butter-and-egg wagons, and milk wagons came by regularly. Ice wagons would stop if you put a card in the window saying 25 or 50 in huge numbers, indicating the number of pounds of ice that you needed. From time to time men with farm wagons would sell apples, or potatoes, or strawberries in season. And occasionally, the rags, bones and bottles collector, or "sheeny," would go by with his ancient horse and decrepit wagon, calling out, "A-rags-a-bones-a-bottles."

Canada Bread wagons carried the proud motto "The loaf that stopped mother baking." Usually someone had scrawled below: "It killed her." Mark Bredin, who built and lived in the big house at 51 Dawlish Avenue, and who built Bredin's Bakery into the huge Canada Bread Company, would hardly have approved.

Most of the horses knew the route and required very little direction from the driver. There is the story of the Eaton's horse that knew his driver was taking too long for coffee at that last house and therefore set off down Yonge Street without him. The driver, by taking a streetcar, was able to catch up with his wagon just below St. Clair.

By the late 1920s a few prosperous homes had installed electric refrigerators, probably the "Frigidaire with a round drum on top — available in white, period." Washing machines were also available, not just the zinc-lined tubs that could be rocked with a long handle, but the real electric-powered washing machines, together with their running mates, the electric "mangle." Old folks shook their heads at this sort of thing, and it would be at least the fifties before such things became common.

In the 1920s and 30s paved roads, sewers, electricity and gas — all the basic services — were being installed or updated. Side streets were paved by a great steam-operated machine that laid down a concrete roadway 14 feet wide. Strips of earth were left on each side to park on, or for the delivery horse to amble on, or, best of all, for the burning of autumn leaves. On a good Saturday morning in October, North Toronto smelled gorgeous.

Bus routes fed the new streetcars. The first of these, in 1921, was the Mt. Pleasant route, which ran east on Merton and which used a trolley bus starting in 1922. Another

In 1923, number 10 Strathallan Boulevard rose in what had hitherto been farmland. The little girl was Lois Leavens, who, nearly 20 years later, would be in the first small contingent of the Canadian Women's Army Corps to go overseas in World War II.

125

early bus route in North Toronto was a Gray Coach Lines double-fare service that went downtown via Avenue Road and Russell Hill Road; it was started in 1925. The Oriole bus route started in 1927, the Eglinton route in 1930, the Lawrence route in 1934.

Some street corners were becoming quite busy and controls of some kind were needed. By 1911 a policeman stood in the centre of the intersection and hand-operated a semaphore that said 'Go' and 'Stop'. Traffic lights as we know them were first installed in Toronto in 1928, but did not reach North Toronto until 1930. However, traffic signals well in advance of their time were installed at Chatsworth and Yonge at that time. At that intersection, the traffic light remained green for Yonge Street traffic until a car on Chatsworth or St. Edmunds honked its horn, or until a pedestrian pressed a button. In today's traffic, one can imagine the chaos if traffic lights could be changed by honking a horn.

Not a day would go by, except Sunday of course, without some North Torontonian driving a brand-new automobile into his driveway to the smiles and envy of his neighbours. Cars were rapidly becoming big business, and they came in a marvellous range of shapes, sizes and prices. There were the names still common today — Fords, Chevrolets, Buicks, Chryslers — and others, like Willys-Knights, Stearns-Knights, Marmons, McLaughlin-Buicks, Graham-Paiges, Moons, Hudsons, Wiltons and Durants. Each was distinctive in some way and this placed a heavy load on the boys of the time, for they felt they had to know each make by year — as well as remembering the name of every horse in the district.

In the 20s and 30s North Toronto became obsessed with the automobile. Service stations threatened to take over almost every street corner. This picture looks north by west at the corner of Oriole Parkway and Eglinton. Four stations on four corners! They varied widely in architecture — the one on the left is quite handsome, but not nearly as cute as the little castle-like edifices built by Joy Oils Limited and owned by Mrs. Austin. However useful these stations were, and however much they indicated the prosperity of the area, can we not shed a tear for the fate of the Gartshore house, once commanding spacious lawns but now cowering under the right side of the big Gasolene sign.

Some of the bigger cars were memorable indeed: the Pierce-Arrow, with its huge headlights moulded into the fenders and a 14,000 cc. 6-cylinder engine; the Packard, with its distinctive radiator and styling. Edward Dewart of Glengrove Avenue drove a massive and stylish 12-cylinder Packard open touring sedan. It would run quietly along at five miles per hour in high gear and yet would accelerate smoothly to whatever speed you wished with no more noise than the rush of air into the carburetors, made possible by a narrow piston with a long stroke. The Essex had a cork-on-steel-in-oil clutch that was remarkably smooth. The Chevrolet 409, the "Baby Grand," had a cone-shaped *leather* clutch; if it started to slip, a pinch of "Fuller's Earth" could be added; if it started to grab, a few drops of oil would have the desired effect.

Unfortunately, most of the cars produced in the 1920s were quite ugly, including the Durant that was manufactured at Leaside (the old head office still stands at 150 Laird Drive), as well as the Hudson and Essex being sold at the corner of Sheldrake and Yonge.

Perhaps clubs best demonstrated prosperity in the 1920s. The Rosedale Golf Club, having moved from Rosedale to its new location overlooking the Don Valley, had built a handsome clubhouse by 1922. It was a flourishing and expensive club. On the other hand, the North Toronto Golf Club, west of Yonge and south of Lawrence, had tried to be an economy-style course and failed.

The Eglinton Hunt Club certainly added social lustre to North Toronto in the 1920s and 30s. The Hunt, of course, was a long-established tradition in Toronto. The first official meet had been held at the Golden Lion Hotel at Yonge and Sheppard in 1843. But by 1909 the Toronto Hunt at Scarborough Bluffs began looking for better hunting country. They felt they had found it near Avenue Road and Eglinton, in spite of the furious expansion of nearby North Toronto.

George W. Beardmore provided the drive and the money needed to create an Eglinton branch of the Toronto Hunt. He remained a Master of the Hunt for 40 years, including 11 years as Master of the Eglinton Hunt. The Gartshore home at Oriole Parkway and Burnaby was bought and remodelled for the club. Two dining rooms were installed, kitchens renovated, and the club initials (T.H.C.) were sandblasted into the glass of the front door, where they remain today. But the initials were soon outdated; by 1922 the club had become the independent Eglinton Hunt Club.

Beardmore didn't stop there. Almost entirely at his own expense he caused to be built "the finest stables and arena to be found anywhere at the time." These buildings were of brick and stone from cellar to weather vane, housed 140 horses, and included "an arena (60' x 300'), washing and clipping corridor, blacksmith shop, kitchen...office

The EGLINTON HUNT CLUB is well recorded in this aerial photograph taken about 1922. The wide road in the foreground is Roselawn Avenue. The narrow one Avenue Road, beginning to poke its way north through farm fields. We are looking southeast; Yonge and Eglinton would be just past the top of the picture.

In the centre is the Eglinton Hunt Club, complete with its excellent stables and outdoor track with bleachers. The main entrance is from Elwood Avenue. Some distance away, the clubhouse stands surrounded by woods at the upper right. Between the clubhouse and the stables long ago, John Montgomery built his house just before the Rebellion of 1837.

The stables of the Eglinton Hunt Club were both attractive and state of the art. The cars of the late 20s may have been state of the art, but to say the least they were rather awkward-looking vehicles.

GEORGE W. BEARDMORE provided the drive and money needed to create an Eglinton branch of the Toronto Hunt Club. His portrait reflects not only something of his personality, but also something of the times when silver buckles on shoes and formal dress breeches were still in style.

tack room, saddle room, lounge (23' x 65') and an outside arena for summer with a grandstand." Later an indoor arena for polo was added. By 1930 the Gartshore clubhouse was replaced by a fine new one at the corner of Avenue Road and Roselawn.

This splendid set-up was said to "allow the humblest of one-horse owners to school their horses conveniently." But there were not many "humble" owners; the Eglinton Hunt was prominent in Toronto society of the time. The Eglinton Hunt actually rode to hounds and hunted. Many older North Torontonians today can recall the horses, the "pink" coats, and the dogs, all sweeping up Avenue Road, then perhaps west on Lawrence into the country, or east towards the big estates at Bayview. It was an exciting sight.

Beardmore died in the early 1930s and the club gradually deteriorated in the face of the Depression. In 1939 the entire estate was sold to the Royal Canadian Air Force. As of 1992 it is a Canadian Forces Staff Training School. The Eglinton Hunt moved and is now located in Caledon Township.

The summer cottage became more common in the 1920s, although wealthy people had built summer homes much earlier, and in many places — some of them on Toronto Island and one at least in the Don Valley at Oriole. Many of those without cottages took their holidays at a summer hotel. Huge, elaborate, and usually white-painted hotels were plentiful north of Toronto: Wawa and Bigwin Inn on the Lake of Bays; Beaumaris, Windermere and the Royal Muskoka on the Muskoka Lakes. But people were beginning to have faith in the automobile, and this opened up many areas not served by trains or the many little steamships that plied the lakes north of Toronto. You could order a cottage by mail direct from Eaton's catalogue: just tell them the location of your lot, pick the cottage of your choice, and by spring it would be ready for occupancy. The Murch family of North Toronto found that Eaton's had faced their new cottage to the wrong

view. It was corrected by building a wide, screened verandah around the entire building — at no extra cost.

If you stayed in the city, there were parks, concerts, Centre Island, Sunnyside, boat trips on the *Cayuga*, the *Northumberland*, or the *Chippewa*. There was one big swimming pool at Sunnyside, and the TTC ran free cars there for children; the North Toronto car waited on a wye at the corner of Glencairn and Yonge. If you didn't want the long streetcar ride, with every kid in the car yelling and waving towels, there was always the Don, where bathing suits were unnecessary. (The fashion in bathing suits in the 1920s was an itchy black wool suit with shoulder straps and circular holes showing the side ribs.) Summer would end soon enough and the children would head back to school.

The first snowfall may have delighted the kids, but it was a hard time for most mothers. All outdoor clothing was made of wool; it got wet; it caught on every projection; and it wore out surprisingly quickly. For most of the winter, drying clothes festooned the basement. (It was a basement if the house was fairly new, but the space beneath older houses was usually called a cellar, with little headroom.)

There were many good hills for tobogganing: Eglinton Park, Sherwood Park, "Aura Lee Hill" (north of Blythwood and east of Mt. Pleasant), the ravine south of Chatsworth, and best of all, Rosedale golf course, which offered a fine collection of slopes of

At the end of Sherwood Avenue in the late 1920s, the city prepared and iced a bobsleigh run that swept down into the lower part of Waterworks Park. Most of the time it served as a toboggan run for younger children, but as a bobsleigh run, it was an exciting adventure until about 1930, when a sleigh hit the parapet of the bridge over Stibbard's Creek and young Jimmy Durham was killed. That was the end of the city-sponsored bob run.

(continued on page 134)   129

THE NORTH TORONTO
SCHOOLS

THE NUMBER and size of schools in North Toronto today demonstrate the current importance of education. It was not always so. It took many years for the idea of schooling to become accepted, as the figures in the chart show (see below). As early as 1807 there was a school in the Don Valley. It was a small log structure that stood just behind the present Jolly Miller Tavern. Such a school would have been built, and the teacher paid, by local donations. Seneca Ketchum seems to have been prominent in this early school, as he was in the case of the first church. Church and school may even have shared the same building.

The first school in the immediate area of North Toronto, however, was built in 1842 at the southwest corner of Yonge and the present St. Clements Avenue. Eight years later it was rebuilt in brick (and still stands, now known as the Orange Hall). It was a time when only half the children spent as much as one year at school; many of the local farmers believed that schooling was just a deterrent to the real work of farming.

In 1845 John Boyd, a sound Toronto scholar, came to teach at Eglinton School. It is fairly safe to assume that he taught beginning reading from the book most commonly used at the time, Murray's *English Reader*. It is hard to imagine a child learning to read from this book, which Charles Phillips, in his book *The Development of Public Education in Canada*, describes as follows: "...pieces in prose and verse selected from the best writers, designed to assist young persons to read with propriety and effect;...The pieces are classified and arranged as narrative, didactic, argumentative, descriptive, and so on.... Opening at random we find such titles as 'The misery of pride,' 'The mortifications of vice greater than those of virtue,'...'A man perishing in the snow; from whence reflections are raised on the miseries of life.'"

In the 1880s the small school at St. Clements and Yonge was replaced by a much larger brick building on Erskine Avenue, the present John Fisher School. In the meantime another school had been operating in the Davisville area. Charles Lea recalled starting school in 1857 in a two-storey

In 1922 ST. CLEMENT'S SCHOOL occupied a former farmhouse standing well back from Yonge Street on the south side of present-day St. Clements Avenue.

Students and teachers posed in front of EGLINTON SCHOOL on Erskine Avenue sometime before 1890.

AVERAGE NUMBER OF MONTHS SPENT IN SCHOOL

1830	1850	1870	1890	1910	1930	1950
5	10	30	35	55	80	90

JOHN FISHER SCHOOL

BEDFORD PARK SCHOOL grew steadily bigger in the 20s and 30s.

JOHN ROSS ROBERTSON SCHOOL was completed in 1921 and still looks the same today.

frame building at the north corner of Balloil and Yonge. A large brick building on Millwood Road just east of Yonge soon followed. By 1892 the new Town of North Toronto had built additions to both the Eglinton and Davisville schools, and in 1911 Bedford Park School was opened. The architectural planning of these schools more than rivalled the local churches as a focus of public attention.

Eglinton School was opened in 1912 at Eglinton and Mt. Pleasant; the earlier Eglinton School on Erskine Avenue was renamed John Fisher School, after North Toronto's long-time mayor. Hodgson School was completed in 1915 and named after William Wastel Hodgson, a former chairman of the Toronto Board of Education. This school had formerly consisted of three portables known as Davisville East School. St. Monica's, the first separate school, opened in 1916. John Ross Robertson operated as four portables as early as 1919. Both Hodgson and John Ross Robertson started out with women principals: Alda Burger in the case of Hodgson, and Annie Cullen for John Ross Robertson. By 1921 the new John Ross Robertson building was completed.

Between 1925 and 1929 three new elementary schools were built and additions were made to six others. In 1928 Maurice Cody School moved from three portables to its permanent building. (The Rev. Canon H.J. Cody was a distinguished Toronto clergyman and educator. His son, Maurice, was a 30-year-old lawyer when he drowned on a camping trip. There was a popular wave of sympathy, and when a friend of the father proposed to name the school after the son, the Board of Education approved.) In Bedford Park West, John Wanless School was opened in 1927, after a year in portables. It was named after a prominent jeweller and former chairman of the Board of Education. One year later Allenby School was opened on Avenue Road, after two years in portables. It was named — perhaps they were running out of names — after a British General from World War I. Meanwhile a portable offshoot of Bedford Park School had been opened in 1927 on Strathgowan Crescent. Five years later Blythwood School was completed and occupied.

Schools were formal and disciplined. Pupils lined up — boys and girls separately — and marched into class. (At John Ross Robertson this march was made memorable by Miss Griffin playing "In an English Country Garden" on the piano.) The great threat to pupils was the strap, which was administered with vigour and was generally approved by parents. It was not uncommon for a parent to say, "If you get the strap at school, you'll get a real licking here at home."

Schoolyards were either of mud or cinders, and many a 70-year-old today can show you cinders ground permanently into his or her knees. Across these yards, the boys sometimes paraded as a cadet corps, carrying roughly-shaped wooden rifles. A few boys were awarded heavy red wool army jackets, and perhaps even a real rifle with the bolt removed. Patriotism was emphasized and popular, and Canada and the British Empire received almost equal emphasis.

Secondary education started in North Toronto in 1910. Some 11 students occupied the second floor of the Town Hall under principal George "Shorty" Reed. A new building, to be known as North Toronto Collegiate (later Collegiate Institute), was opened two years later on Roehampton Avenue east of Yonge. Attendance at high school was not just a matter of choice, there were province-wide entrance examinations at the end of senior fourth, now known as grade eight.

During the 1920s the percentage of pupils attending high school doubled, and the traditional academic view of education was broadened. This resulted in the opening in 1930 of a major new institution called Northern Vocational School, which aimed at a more practical education for those who did not plan a university career. In the first year Northern enrolled 529 students. There remained a lingering feeling that Northern was a sort of blue-collar school, and North Toronto Collegiate continued to have so many pupils that they occupied the northern wing of Northern Vocational in the early thirties. Steps were taken to provide additional facilities for the so-called academic stream, and the result was Lawrence Park Collegiate, opened in 1936 with an enrolment of 648 students.

On almost any weekday in the 1910s, a more-than-dignified lady in a cape could be seen walking up the west side of Yonge Street from Roselawn to St. Clements Avenue. This was Mrs. Constance Waugh, the principal of St. Clements School. More than anyone else, Mrs. Waugh set the tone and character of this small private day-school that had become a North Toronto institution. Begun in 1911 in the Parish Hall of St. Clements Church, it has endured rather than grown, while dispensing education that is perhaps a little more dignified than that offered by the public schools. (Originally, it was co-educational, and there is still a men's branch of the Old Girls' Association.) Despite its unprepossessing campus on St. Clements just west of Yonge, it maintains a solid and well-deserved local tradition.

In the mid-1920s a larger and more broadly based private school for girls came to North Toronto. Havergal College moved from its main building on Jarvis Street (later the home of the CBC), and from its small offshoot on St. Clair Avenue just west of Yonge, to a handsome new campus on Avenue Road just south of Lawrence. This was an Anglican school providing tuition and boarding for girls from many countries, as did Loretto Abbey, a

MAURICE CODY SCHOOL opened in 1928.

JOHN WANLESS SCHOOL with the newer style school yard common today.

ALLENBY SCHOOL now stands where an Indain village stood 500 years ago.

HAVERGAL COLLEGE campus on Avenue Road just south of Lawrence.

Catholic private school for girls which was built about the same time but just outside what can really be considered as North Toronto. Both schools were considered to be finishing schools for young ladies. There was even an approved way to sit: slightly angled on the chair, knees together, feet on the floor, with one foot about four inches ahead of the other, hands folded loosely in the lap — now, alas, forgotten in a splay of blue jeans!

Private schools for boys were less than successful in North Toronto. In 1913 St. Clement's College for Boys occupied the old Doel home on Blythwood Road a block east of Yonge, but by 1919 it had moved from North Toronto to 1545 Bathurst Street (where it still operated in 1935). Another boys' school was started by Norval Waddington early in the 1920s. For a time it operated at 21 Deloraine Avenue, but moved to the old Jarvis home at the northeast corner of Lawrence and Yonge. It was closed about 1935. •

The "Moff" at LAWRENCE PARK COLLEGIATE… "probably 1947. This was the BIG SPRING DANCE and probably only one girl might dare to ask a boy to attend. Jeans in those days were for farmers only, and since this was the send-off for students who went to work on farms (and thereby avoided final exams), jeans were the rig-of-the-day for Moffers. Usually, in 1947-48, the boy wore good slacks, and the girls wore tunics or skirts with blouses and sweaters. The sweaters, if cardigans, were worn buttoned down the back and always with a string of pearls."

CHRISTINE JOHNSON

mixed difficulty, including one that dropped almost straight down from the clubhouse. Teenagers were usually gregarious enough to visit several of these hills, looking for friends or perhaps attractive members of the opposite sex.

Skiing would become popular later in the thirties, but until then the most exciting winter sport was bobsleighing. At Sherwood Park, as the picture shows, the City Parks Department built a bob-run that provided a rather spectacular ride. A bobsleigh was simply two sleighs mounted at either end of a long, sturdy plank. The steersman sat at the front with his feet on the front sleigh and with ropes to aid in steering. Passengers sat tightly in behind him, but the last one on usually lay down on the end of the plank. On an icy run, the speeds were terrific, fast enough to be dangerous. The Sherwood bob-run was closed down about 1930, when a sleigh hit the parapet of the bridge over Stibbard's Creek and an unfortunate lad named Jimmy Durham was killed.

A good deal of hand labour was needed to supplement this steam-powered concrete-laying machine as it paved Keewatin Avenue. McMurtry's grocery was at the northeast corner of Keewatin and Yonge. Note that the west side of Yonge Street is still an open field.

Skating was very popular. A large pleasure rink surrounded a hockey "cushion" behind the stores between Roselawn and Castlefield. The North Toronto Band played there two evenings a week. Adults and children circled counterclockwise to tunes like the "Skater's Waltz." Many kinds of skates were in use, from "bobskates" for the very young, through the new "tube skates," and even a few sets of "speeders" with long 16-inch blades. Hockey cushions were set up each winter in the schoolyards, and the *thunk* of the puck against the boards proved to be a distinctive and memorable sound.

Spring was the time for playing marbles in the melting snow and mud. The little streams of North Toronto had not yet been tamed and funnelled into storm sewers. As the snow melted, these streams carried a great deal of water, more than could be handled by the iron conduits built under the roads. Some large bodies of water were dammed up. The late Dr. Keith described the small lake that formed north and west of Lawrence and Yonge. He and his sister built a raft that carried them — he swore — to lodge against the roof of an almost submerged privy. Similar ponds formed at Mt. Pleasant and Broadway, and at Eglinton and Bayview. Another creek crossed Avenue Road just south of Glencairn and ran down through a valley to Pears Park, thence southwesterly to Merton and Mt. Pleasant, creating ponds as it went. The present sports field of Lawrence Park Collegiate was a steep valley that was dammed by the local kids and used as a rink in the winter (it was a great mess of old planks, rocks, and water in the spring). That same valley on the north side of Lawrence Avenue, the present site of Sylvan Valleyway, was a dump filled with ugly refuse and inhabited by sewer rats. The use of air rifles and well-thrown rocks never seemed to reduce the rat population.

These valleys provided, and still provide, some very scenic spots. The lawn bowling club in the valley where Lytton and Alexandra come together must be one of the most picturesque sights in North Toronto; it was established at a very early date. Across Lytton from that location is a little city park that was formerly the garden of "Glenburn," home of the Begg family, later the home of the Foster Hewitts. Long-time neighbours recall a wedding that filled this garden bowl with ladies in huge garden-party hats, long white gloves, and the summery chiffon dresses of the period.

But lest we think of the twenties as one great garden party, we should recall the other side of the coin. Just downstream, south again from the Begg's valley garden, a young girl was found abused and dead. In the valley behind John Ross Robertson School, a boy, while playing, ate some water hemlock and died in the hospital. At Yonge and Sheldrake a man got off a late streetcar and was shot and killed on the spot. Next morning, the only sign of the tragedy was a patch of sawdust on the gravel of the service station. The most dramatic episode of this kind was the "Lilac Bush Murder," which took place on Blythwood Road. At the top of the rise, just west of Bayview, there had been a farmhouse surrounded by lilac bushes. When the house was pulled down, the lilacs remained and enclosed a little area quite suitable for trysts. One such tryst proved fatal, and a girl's body was found there the next day. It remains an unsolved mystery.

During the 1920s one of the greatest social changes in history began for North Toronto. In 1922, if you had a crystal set radio, and if you listened carefully, you could hear voices coming over the air from CFCA, Toronto's first radio station, operated by the Toronto *Star*. It was the beginning of a great movement by which radio and then television brought other people and other parts of the world into the home. No longer did you need to wait and read about it, you could hear it actually happening! In the late twenties, in North Toronto, it was the height of excitement to listen to the radio and hear the finish of the great CNE Swimming Races. By 1925 a Torontonian named Edward Sammuel "Ted" Rogers had developed a radio that simply plugged in, and radio soon became quite common. (The RB in CFRB derived from "Roger's Batteryless.") Sunday sermons on the radio were very important in the early days. The JBC in CJBC stood for Jarvis Street Baptist Church, and thousands of Torontonians were soon listening to the sermons of the Reverend T.T. Shields.

Times were prosperous and income taxes were light. Envious eyes were cast on estates like "Sunnybrook Farm," and two pairs of eyes in particular marked out the area on Bayview just north of "Sunnybrook." Dr. Herbert Bruce and his English bride often rode their horses up the dirt road that was Bayview Avenue. They were attracted to the

Sir Clifford and Lady Sifton in front of their Lawrence Avenue home.

136

old farm where generations of Joneses had spent 90 years. The house stood on the edge of the valley, reached by a splendid lane of cedars. Upon enquiry, someone thought it was owned by Sir Henry Pellatt. Sir Henry, when phoned, didn't know whether or not he owned it, but said that he would consider a deal if he did. It proved that he did, and the deal was made. In 1920, on the actual foundation of the old Jones house, arose a handsome English-style home named "Annandale," after the castle owned by ancestor Robert Bruce in Scotland centuries ago. It was designed by Eden Smith, whose best-known work is probably the Old Mill on the Humber.

The Honourable Herbert A. Bruce, M.D., F.A.C.S., L.R.C.P., F.R.C.S. (Eng.), was a self-made man. He started as a farm boy on the muddy banks of Lake Scugog, and by hard work and intelligence, he reached a notable position in medical circles and finally attained to the highest position open in Ontario in 1932, when he was appointed Lieutenant-Governor of the province. Dr. Bruce's life was always on the way up, it seems. After ten years at "Annandale" he felt he needed more room and therefore moved to Steeles and Bayview, and out of this story. So that he would remember the old lot fondly, before leaving he sold two pieces of the property for $60,000 each, and the remainder, with the house, for a much greater sum.

"GLENDON HALL," the home of E.R. Wood, was one of the big houses built on Bayview between Blythwood Road and Lawrence in the 20s. The estate was donated to the university by the family and became the campus of Glendon College.

The superb settings on the edges of the Don Valley soon became very popular. In 1923 Edward Rogers Wood, known as E.R., built an especially fine home just to the east of the junction of Bayview and Lawrence. (For many years Bayview took a winding way down the steep hill to the east of its surveyed line; this is used today for access to the lower parking lot of Glendon College.) Wood's estate was called "Glendon Hall"; it had beautiful gardens to complement the striking view over the valley. Wood was a leading Toronto financier, vice-president of National Trust, the Bank of Commerce, Canada Life Assurance, and of Brazilian Traction, the predecessor of today's giant Brascan. After his death, his wife, Agnes Euphemia (Smart) Wood, gave the estate to the University of Toronto, which in turn gave it to York University.

In the meantime, in 1930, another beautiful house was built on Wood's property, a house called "Cheddington," very visible on the east side of Bayview just south of the bridge. It was Wood's gift to his daughter and her husband, Murray Fleming. It is said that the same plans were used to build a suitable summer home in Muskoka for the Flemings. (This is offered as an economy tip for the reader!)

At almost the same time as "Glendon Hall" was built, a famous Canadian came to Toronto and built homes for himself and his family on Lawrence Avenue. Sir Clifford Sifton had been a cabinet minister in Sir Wilfred Laurier's government. More than anyone else, he had been responsible for bringing tens of thousands of settlers from

Britain and from Central Europe to populate the Canadian prairies. He had resigned from the government on a matter of principle and had come to Toronto. There, he built three large houses that still stand on the north side of Lawrence just west of Bayview, plus a huge aerodrome-like building that stood for many years beside the Bayview bridge, where the Siftons trained and exercised their horses.

Sifton seems to have avoided the chicanery in land and railways that characterized his predecessors in the 1880s. The Sifton family was well-to-do, with important newspapers and other holdings in the West. J.W. Dafoe, in his biography of Sifton, presents an

intriguing story of the family's move from Ottawa to Toronto: "He and his two sons went to the Ottawa Trust Company offices, where securities were deposited, with two suitcases and a trunk: the securities were 'shovelled' in; the trio and their unusual baggage took the train to Toronto, where the vaults of another trust company opened to receive them."

Three of Sir Clifford's sons had notable careers. Harry Sifton was the chief executive officer of the Sifton family holding company. Clifford Sifton became a barrister, joined the army, was wounded three times in World War I, and was awarded the D.S.O. He became Joint Master of the Toronto and North York Hunt. Wilfred Victor Sifton came out

"DONNINGDVALE'"was built in 1927 by J. J. Vaughan in the English style to fit well into its park-like setting on the edge of the ravine. Today the house is used as a specialized clinic.

of World War I as a major, and in World War II, served for two years as Master-General of Ordnance for the Canadian Army. He later became president of the Canadian Press Association and chancellor of the University of Manitoba.

Three other big houses were also built on Bayview during the twenties and thirties. In 1927 J.J. Vaughan bought property from Dr. Bruce and built a fine home, "Donningvale," on the edge of the ravine. It was built of grey stone, in the English style, and may have fitted into its setting better than any of the other big homes in the area. Vaughan was Sir John Eaton's right-hand man in operating the great department store and its scores of subsidiary enterprises. He was a founding member of the Toronto Art Gallery (now AGO), and a director of Maple Leaf Gardens and the Bank of Toronto. He and his wife were active members in many charitable organizations and service clubs, especially after losing a son in World War II. However, after his death, the house was boarded up and was soon out of sight in its great park. It is said that one of the founders of the Renascent movement spent some time in Sunnybrook Hospital, and while a walking convalescent, saw this fine old deserted house. Fortunately, today it is part of the Renascent Centres movement.

In the late 1920s David Dunkelman of Tip Top Tailors lived with his family in the former Kilgour "Sunnybrook" house. In 1930 Edgar Eaton built a major home on the south side of Blythwood Road, in the valley about 200 yards west of Bayview Avenue. It stands today, subdivided into several apartments. Originally, it was reached from Blyth-wood, and the chauffeur's lodge and garage, fronted by a low stone wall, has become 539 Blythwood. The gardener's cottage, down closer to the house, had a most picturesque dovecote. This has become an attractive residence on Sunnydene Crescent.

Just south of Vaughan's house, James Stanley McLean had a home built on the edge of the ravine. "Bayview" was a Scottish baronial home of Canadian fieldstone. Together with its garage and coach house, it presents a fine sight at the end of a long, winding drive from Bayview Avenue. McLean started as a clerk in a small abattoir and ended up as the president of Canada Packers. He was a man of drive and intelligence who disliked unions but treated his employees to travelling exhibits of fine art. He was not hindered by his marriage to a niece of Sir Joseph Flavelle.

The architect of "Bayview" was Eric Arthur, a New Zealander who made major con-tributions to the history and development of Canadian architecture. He lived in North Toronto, building a house on Weybourne Crescent which was arguably the most out-of-place home in Lawrence Park. But the house he built for McLean is delightful. Fort-unately, it can be seen today much as it was in the thirties, since it is used for receptions and weddings, under the general administration of Sunnybrook Health Centre.

The most impressive of the big Bayview houses was built for Alfred Rogers, who had bought Dr. Bruce's "Annandale" estate. Bruce had built on the foundation of the Jones farmhouse; now Rogers built on the same foundation, spending, it is said, $250,000 Depression dollars on improvements to the house alone. Up rose a Jacobean castle call-

The Eglinton Hunt was a notable sight as it cantered up an unpaved Avenue Road, complete with hounds "giving tongue" and riders in red coats. The coats of the Eglinton Hunt had lapel facings of Copenhagen blue; this distinguished them from members of other Toronto hunt clubs.

ed "Uplands," together with gardens and stables (although the main Rogers stables were at his country seat at Lake Simcoe). Rogers was an active man — president of Canada Building Materials, St. Mary's Cement, and Elias Rogers Coal and Oil. He was a director of Maple Leaf Gardens, Ridley College and the Wellesley Hospital; a governor of the University of Toronto; honourary president of the Royal Agricultural Winter Fair; vice-president of the Canadian National Exhibition; and Joint Master of the Toronto Hunt!

"Alf" Rogers knew how to do things well. *Mayfair* magazine, for example, reported in 1930 that "Mr. Alfred Rogers' luncheon reached a peak of recherche where it may with every reason be termed the most important stag party given anywhere in Canada." This took place in the Crystal Ballroom of the King Edward Hotel.

After the almost frenzied building and moving of the 1920s, North Toronto settled down a bit. Many, perhaps most, of the new homes were owned by married couples who sought a good place to raise a family. They hardly expected the Great Depression of the thirties. Nevertheless they met it with resignation rather than protest — not for North Torontonians the hunger marches of less fortunate Canadians. Not long ago a woman said that the Depression did not really affect North Toronto. In this she was wrong. Perhaps *her* parents had been unaffected, or more likely, she had been too young to remember. Children obviously live the life of the moment, and most elderly people can take anything that fate sends them; it was young and middle-age adults that took the strain of the Depression.

The collapse of the stock market in late 1929 was serious enough to cause a few suicides in North Toronto. One poor man, burning with despair, threw himself off the Yonge Boulevard Bridge, but succeeded only in breaking his legs in the mud of the Don. He did not try again. (The Yonge Boulevard Bridge had been built in 1929 to by-pass the York Mills Hollow and its icy slopes. The bridge was reached from Yonge Boulevard. It is now used to carry Highway 401 across the valley.)

The economy slowed down, but it did not shut down. The 1933 model cars sold quite successfully, and they had a certain elegance of design lacking in models of the years before and after. Automobiles were a godsend at the time: Canada was the world's second-largest exporter of cars. General Motors, Ford of Canada, and Chrysler were busy and prosperous, and their increasing size allowed them to take over or drive out of business the many small companies that operated in the 1920s. On the North Toronto part of Yonge Street, there were six garages and one "horseshoer" in 1914; in 1937 there were 38 gas stations, 11 per mile, and 11 car sales agencies.

There were visible signs of the Depression — the odd store closed down, some houses were left unoccupied, snow went unshovelled, lawns uncut — but North Toronto was more fortunate than most parts of Canada at a time when hundreds of thousands were out of work, and when downtown St. Lawrence Hall provided disinfectant and steel cots for hundreds of drifters. There was little protest in North Toronto, a traditionally stable Liberal or Conservative community. The voting pattern was simple. From the time of Confederation in 1867 until 1891 North Toronto voted Liberal, as did the other rural areas of York County. James Metcalfe had three terms in office, followed by Alexander Mackenzie with three terms. Mackenzie, leader of the Liberal Party, had been Canada's second Prime Minister (1873-78) and seems to have chosen this as a safe riding. But an increasing number of urban residents in North Toronto eventually swayed the vote in the direction of the Conservatives, who had dominated the city since the Rebellion of 1837. The riding elected William Findlay MacLean, the publisher of the *Toronto World* in 1896. It remained Conservative under such men as Richard Baker and Donald Fleming, with one brief exception, until well into the 1960s.

The thirties saw an increasing sense of social awareness. In 1930, for example, there was agitation in Parliament for the introduction of unemployment insurance. At that time the Minister of Labour replied that "unemployment insurance will be adopted...only after public opinion has been educated to the necessity for such legislation." Within five years that education had taken place, and in 1935 the first measure of unemployment insurance was passed into law. (It did not, however, cover those hundreds of thousands already unemployed.) But in the same year laws were passed relating to the 48-hour week, a day of rest every seven days, and even the first minimum-wage legislation. There was a weak attempt at federal welfare, giving 25 cents per child per week where real need existed!

Social awareness was in the air, and the underprivileged were being looked at in a new light — sometimes with contradictory results. In the late 1920s the bank at Lawrence and Yonge was robbed by what was called the Red Ryan Gang. Soon after, Ryan was caught and sent to prison at Kingston. While there, he showed a complete change of character, which pleased those who believed that most criminals were unfortunates whose background had not given them a chance to go straight. Ryan's remarkable transformation caught the public eye, as did his statement, "Tell those young men who are slipping backwards on life's highway to keep to the straight and narrow." Prime Minister R.B. Bennett himself came from Ottawa to Kingston to meet this important convert. A special parole was arranged. Ryan returned to Toronto, where he was welcomed with open arms and given work that paid him a good annual salary. He was entertained by civic and social leaders. A writer named Roy Greenaway, who lived on Lytton Boulevard, co-authored a manuscript on this transformation of a criminal. On May 23, 1936, there was an armed robbery in Sarnia. In the ensuing confrontation, a policeman and two robbers were shot and killed. One of the dead was Red Ryan, the new pillar of righteousness! There were red faces and a great many disappointed people. The book, so hopefully conceived, was never published.

Social awareness was fine, but there was a crying need to get away from the Depression, to lose oneself in something a little more romantic. The movies provided some of this relief.

If there was one business that came through the Depression even better than the automotive business, it was the movies. Prior to becoming part of the city, the North Toronto council had turned down requests to open a movie theatre in the area. But sometime around 1912 the city permitted the opening of two theatres close together

CAPITOL

The left side of this picture shows the break between the Capitol theatre and the Capitol building, which was built in front of the theatre three of four years later. On the second floor, Drs. Sirrs and Evans attended to North Toronto's teeth for many years. In the main-floor corner florist shop was Stan Muston, well-known and affable, whose father operated a greenhouse in the Davisville area at the turn of the century. This picture shows a microcosm of men's headwear in the 1920s. Starting at the left are two men in cloth caps — a sure sign of the working man; then a gentleman wearing a derby; beside him a fedora in the conservative level-brim style; by the streetcar stop is a fedora worn more rakishly; and in front of the foyer are two men wearing Homburgs. The sole woman perhaps ponders the newest shade of rayon stockings or the latest in garter belts.

PANORAMIC VIEW

PANORAMIC CAMERA CO.
TORONTO

TOM MIX   TOM MIX IN THE CANYON OF LIGHT

2496 STERLING HOSIERY MILLS 2496

R2518.
PANORAMIC CAMERA Co.
TORONTO.

in the centre of North Toronto. The Royal was on Yonge between Roselawn and Castlefield and seated 300 in a building that had a 25-foot frontage on Yonge. There was a foyer with glazed swinging doors, a centre aisle, and a ladder that allowed the operator to climb up to his little box. The Royal went out of business in 1917. The York, later known as the York Eglinton, was just north of Castlefield on Yonge. The northwest corner of Castlefield was vacant, the Zion Baptist Church having been moved from there to the south side of Castlefield. The York Theatre was on the next lot to the north. It seated 378. At the front of the theatre was a small pit for the pianist, and at the back, a ladder for the operator. The seats, one man recalls, were simply kitchen chairs in rows. There was a small foyer with the ticket wicket in the centre. The York Eglinton stayed in business until 1922, after which it was replaced by a new theatre, the Capitol.

The Capitol was the first big theatre in the area. It was built by a Mr. McClelland, who had come from Kingston, Jamaica, to make his fortune. The Capitol Building, as it appears today, was built in two stages. The actual theatre was built first, about 30 feet back from Yonge Street. A little store had been built right at the corner of Castlefield, and it remained untouched with the theatre behind it. In 1924-25 a three-storey building was erected in front of the theatre and enclosing the little shop on the corner.

The Capitol was successful from the start. Through most of the 1920s the pictures were black-and-white, and of course silent. The theatre provided a pianist to accompany these silent pictures. The pianist was a person of infinite adaptability who sat below the screen, playing continuously and in total darkness, and adapting her or his music to the needs of the story, changing key, style and tempo effortlessly. Throughout the twenties, Charlie Chaplin, Douglas Fairbanks, and Toronto's own Mary Pickford were among the top stars, but the highest paid of all was Tom Mix, as the cowboy movies swept America and then the world.

The Saturday matinee was always crowded with kids coming back to see how Pauline could escape from the perils in which she had been left last week. Almost everyone seemed to have the 10 cents for a ticket. The pianist was moved to the side, out of range of assorted missiles and abuse. Roars, boos, whistling, and paper water-bombs greeted unpopular events or villains; there was violent audience participation. Periodically, the picture would be stopped, and Mr. Maude, the theatre's general factotum, would point out that the picture would continue only if there was reasonable silence. Eventually, the noise would die down, the floors would be mopped up, and Tom Mix could continue to capture the bad guys, and perhaps even win a shy kiss from the heroine.

The Capitol was followed by the Bedford and Belsize (1928), the Hudson (1930), the Circle (1933) and the Eglinton (1937). All were soon busy. In 1928 the *Jazz Singer* introduced talkies to North Toronto, and soon there followed a stream of musicals like *Rio Rita* and *Broadway Melody*. The main film was preceded by several short films. First came the Movietone News, billed as "The Eyes and Ears of the World." The news was followed by a cartoon, then a brief travel film, taken in some beautiful setting, and finally the main film. (By the 1950s television was reducing filmgoers. In 1954 the Belsize became the Crest, a playhouse; in 1966, a movie house again; in 1985, a playhouse; and in 1988, a movie house, the Regent.)

For those who stayed home, there were records to be played on the gramophone, or the phonograph, or the Victrola. In its early years the phonograph was primarily concerned with fairly "high-brow" music. Popular music would come later, but meanwhile the recorded sounds of Caruso or the New York Philharmonic were heard in many North Toronto homes.

Instant sounds from a distance were the gifts of radio. Radio was exciting. Radio developed the concept of the weekly or even daily programs, and soon days and nights were filled with the likes of the Happy Gang, Amos and Andy, the Shadow, Fred Allen and Jack Benny. Audiences were held spellbound. (It was years later that Marshall McLuhan pointed out the radio was a "hotter" medium than television, demanding a concentration that television does not.)

The thirties also saw the rise of the big bands. Made popular by radio, these swing bands had the same hold over people as do rock groups today. When Tommy Dorsey, with an unbelievably young Frank Sinatra, came to play at the "Ex," tickets were in high demand. Nearly all of the big bands came to Toronto. Glen Gray stayed long enough to name his band after Casa Loma. North Torontonians could hear excellent local bands as well — Bert Niosi at the Palais Royale at Sunnyside or Ferde Mowry at the Embassy ("Canada's largest dance-hall on springs"). They could even go as far as the Brant Inn in Burlington for an evening of dancing under the stars to Mart Kenny and his Genial Western Gentlemen. •

SOCIAL   NOTES   FROM   THE   SMART   SET

AFTER THE SHOW, we motored out to York Mills...from the sublime to the ridiculous to commit a bromide!... and supped and danced a bit at the *Jolly Miller*, which is a new tea house and 'night club' for Toronto's north end. Our host was Mr. William E. Cox, who is trying to put this new dancing place over in a smart way. The wayside inn at the very bottom of *Hogg's Hollow* hardly knows itself these days! After seventy-two years of plebeian usage it has become a rendezvous with a delightful early-Canadian atmosphere. The walls are hung with bits of Canadiana whose history is intimately associated with the district; the furniture is French Provencal in style, and the window hangings are of a quaintly colourful fabric resembling hand-loomed wools. It was a night of silver moonshine, and from the eastern windows, we peered over the Hollow to the shadow of the hill through which pioneers of York travelled in the days of old Yonge Street... and there eerie thoughts of the 'gang' cached in the nearby swamp which periodically waylaid the unwary as they travelled to and from the Town of York...some six miles distant, and then separated from York Mills proper by some half-dozen struggling settlements. Talk about your Atmosphere! No wonder the *Jolly Miller* is intriguing!

MAYFAIR 1936

THE NORTH TORONTONIANS

B Y 1939 NORTH TORONTO seemed to be just about filled up. Some 60,000 people lived within the municipal limits. Housing continued to spread east toward Bayview and west toward Bathurst. North Toronto's earlier independence as a town was by now almost forgotten; it had become very much a part of Toronto. Most of the old localisms, like the North Toronto Band, had gently faded away. The citizens thought of themselves as Torontonians, but perhaps a little more refined than the rest of the city. (In this they were not alone.)

Yonge Street and the streetcars tied it firmly to the city. There were several little neighbourhoods, usually centred on local shopping areas. These shopping areas are almost exactly the same today as they were in 1939; three of them on Yonge (Davisville to just past Manor, Broadway to Sheldrake, and Ranleigh to Snowdon); one on Mt. Pleasant Road (Belsize to Hillsdale); one on Avenue Road (north from Brookdale); one on Bayview (Millwood to just past Manor); and one on Eglinton (Oriole Parkway and west).

Single-family homes predominated. The goal was to live in a new free-standing house. Some families had to make do in a semi-detached; some even had to live in what had been a farm or turn-of-the-century house. There was no pride in old buildings at the time. The 1828 Snyder farmhouse at 744 Duplex was just another old house broken into apartments. There were also apartments above stores on Yonge and Mt. Pleasant, and apartment buildings were being constructed in increasing numbers. The first apartment building was built in 1916 at Belsize and Yonge, and by the thirties there were quite distinguished apartments like the Lawrence Park Manor and the Du Maurier north of Lawrence.

It was a time of chain stores or groceterias. There was nearly always a Loblaws, an A&P, or a Stop-and-Shop within easy walking distance. Shopping tended to be a daily event and was usually done on foot, although some grocers, like Atkinsons or Eddingtons, would make daily deliveries. Alvar Simpson's shop resembled today's supermarkets. His store was huge and held not only groceries, but also an independent butcher, baker and drugstore under the same roof. Simpson called it the Miracle Marketeria, but unfortunately it was caught in the Depression and ultimately closed. The building

remains, in 1990, as Parkwood Motors on Yonge just north of Montgomery. (Across the street was another notable building of the time, a garage built by Fisher and Ramsay. At the time of building, it was the largest garage under one roof in Canada. It is currently destined to be replaced by condominiums.)

Shopping other than food shopping was centred on the block between Roselawn and Castlefield. That block boasted a Woolworths and a Kresge's (their first in Canada). These stores carried an astounding range of items at very low prices. One could shop for such varied items as jewellery, tropical fish, hot dogs, rayon stockings, or assorted hardware. In that same block was one of the early Loblaw stores, together with Unser's Catering. The latter catered to local weddings — just about the only time that most North Toronto families would go all out. Unser's ice cream was too rich to be eaten in quantity. There was also a Honey Dew restaurant.

There were only half a dozen small restaurants in North Toronto at the time. Most

GODFREY MUNGER, shown here with his daughter, owned the Bedford Park Lunch and Ice Cream Parlour. Inside, the inevitable Coca Cola signs are given real competition by the polished handles of the soda fountain. Ice cream sodas, David Harum sundaes and banana splits were popular treats of the time.

of them provided good family-style food, but people just did not eat out very much in those days; restaurants were patronized mostly by people who didn't have time to go home for meals. A North Toronto housewife would have felt peculiar taking her family out to eat. Snacks with a friend while shopping, however, were socially acceptable. Places like Honey Dew or Hunt's or small local tearooms provided sandwiches, sundaes and chocolate eclairs.

The unrelenting chore of preparing three home-cooked meals a day was the fate of most women in the 1930s and 40s. Ann Morrow Lindbergh referred to these housewives as "the great vacationless." Eating out was very special, probably downtown, and dressed to the teeth. Perhaps they would go to the Savarin on Bay Street, or if father was being thrifty, to Child's, where all you could eat cost 69 cents (needless to say there was a lot of bragging among the young as to how many helpings were eaten).

A look at the directory for North Toronto in 1939 shows that well over 90 percent of the families were of English, Irish, Scottish or German extraction, thus maintaining about the same ethnic mix as the settlers of 1800. It was a community that was proud of the British Commonwealth and almost fiercely devoted to British royalty. When the young King George VI and Queen Elizabeth came to Toronto in 1939, the city rose to greet them. We know that north-end schoolchildren were among the 75,000 pupils who sang at the great reception at Riverdale Park, and we can be sure that many North Tor-

By 1939 North Toronto had some rather handsome apartment buildings, like those at Chatsworth and Yonge. This picture was taken in July, and the patriotic flags were in honour of a visit by the King and Queen. The Supertest station shows two kinds of gas pumps. The older one holds gasoline in a high glass tank. There were marks on the glass to indicate gallons as the gas ran into the car's tank.

onto adults were among the 100,000 others who stood on the hillside and cheered themselves hoarse. When the mounted guard of the Governor General's Horse Guards, in their scarlet uniforms, escorted their Majesties' carriage into the park, it was a ceremony as stirring as most Canadians would ever see. The flags were mostly Union Jacks; it would be many years before Canada had a flag of its own.

The flags flying for the Royal visit would soon fly in another cause. War in Europe was imminent, as the totalitarian states continued on their predatory ways. Back in 1914 many people looked upon war as a "rebuke to the sloth of soft living of modern life." But after the terrible loss of life in the Great War just 20 years earlier, Canada was not prepared to go to war automatically. However, reports of Nazi death camps, the machine-gunning of unarmed Abyssinians, and the burning to death of Spanish villagers in their own church gave pause to even the most pacific. To a Christian nation — and Canada *was* a Christian nation at that time — this was intolerable. The Canadian Parliament voted for war with only one "nay" and there can be no doubt that the people of North Toronto supported this decision.

The war came as no surprise. European armies and navies were poised for action. In Britain, civilian planning had been going on for months. At the outbreak of the war, in four days, 4,000 British trains carried one and a half million children, and the mothers of those in arms, to the countryside, where they would be safe from bombing. Many children were destined to be sent to Canada for safety. For North Toronto, one of the first results of the war was the arrival of British children to be adopted for the duration. And the first sign of the savagery of war was the sinking of the liner *Athenia*, carrying not only adults (including North Torontonians) but scores of children crossing the ocean to security.

There was, of course, a general mobilization in Canada, including the Queen's York Rangers, the local militia unit. As militia, the men were available only for local service, but most of them volunteered for overseas service. Some were transferred to combat units, others went overseas on special assignments; Douglas Goldie spent three years in England while still officially enrolled in the Rangers. There was some local overreaction at first; soldiers with rifles stood 24 hours a day guarding the Glengrove Hydro substation. But in general Canada moved fairly smoothly into the war, probably because virtually everyone opposed the Nazi regime.

Right from the start, women were determined to be active in the war. The pledge of support by the Sir John Beverly Robinson Chapter of the Imperial Order of the Daughters of the Empire exemplified not only the IODE but a great many other women's organizations. Meeting at the Sheldrake Boulevard Preventorium, the women announced strong support for the war effort and pressed for the full participation of women. Voluntary registration of women for war work began almost immediately. At Ottawa, confronted with a formidable letter from a women's group, a mandarin jokingly pleaded that there wasn't enough khaki for men's trousers, let alone *skirts*. It was not funny. Women persevered and soon they were a vital part of every area of the war effort — in the Army's CWACs, the Navy's WRENS, the Air Force's WAAFs. A few women

NATIONAL REGISTRATION
OF WOMEN IN CANADA
Sept. 14 to Sept. 19, 1942
THOSE WHO MUST REGISTER

WHERE YOU MUST REGISTER

THE DATE OF REGISTRATION

THOSE WHO
NEED NOT REGISTER

Recycling is no recent invention. Here is the "blue box" of World War II with its legend: "Don't! throw it away. Throw it at Hitler." The picture shows HOWARD GERBER'S Red Indian service station at Yonge and Cranbrooke about 1943.

were actually accepted into positions of importance in the governmental power strucure. Mrs. Clara Brunke of Teddington Park was made a member of a powerful wartime comittee called the Mayor's Commission of Power. Mrs. Brunke was the president of the Local Council of Women and represented a great many women's organizations and clubs.

Women played a crucial role in wartime industry. On billboards and in magazine ads "Rosie the Rivetter" promoted women's work in areas normally reserved for men. Closer to North Toronto, Research Enterprises in Leaside grew into a huge complex largely staffed by women. The company manufactured critical and complicated range-finders, prismatic gun-sights, and radar. The Eglinton East bus line from Yonge to Brentcliffe was hectically busy as shift workers maintained round-the-clock production. (As a small side issue, Eglinton Avenue ended at Brentcliffe at that time. A dirt track led down into the ravine, where clay had been dug for bricks, but what had once been a ford through the Don was no longer usable in the 1940s.) Special war work of some undetermined nature was done in the big, brick, barnlike building in the valley of Sunnybrook Park. Special research and training related to high-level flying was carried out by the RCAF

Institute of Aviation Medicine at what had been the Hunt Club at Avenue Road and Roselawn.

For North Toronto it was a waiting war, although most of the people contributed in some way, whether through knitting for the troops, or working in war industries, or buying war bonds. This form of raising money was pursued very actively and very successfully. Eglinton Park served as a focal point for raising public interest. The North Toronto Lions Club held springtime carnivals. The Bayview Riding and Driving Association (!) staged a special meet there in 1943. The Army, brought a squadron of tanks down from Camp Borden. Trucks and buses carried huge signs saying things like "Keep the Nazi Heel out of Canada" and North Torontonians were very much aware of Bob Hope's visit to Toronto in 1944 to promote the sale of war stamps. Senior high-school students, to their delight, were given time off to help with farm work before rejoining classes after the harvest. This Toronto Farm Commando Brigade owed much to the direction of Alderman John Innes of Merton Avenue. The costs of the program were absorbed by Eaton's, Simpsons, and the Motion Picture Theatres Association. It was a popular and successful operation; a special letter of appreciation came from MPP George S. Henry, who began his political career in the Township Council at Eglinton, and who would become Premier of Ontario.

The Wartime Prices and Trade Board at Ottawa was very effective in controlling not only prices but the supply of essential materials. Gasoline rationing was introduced in 1941. New cars were virtually unobtainable. Rubber for tires was a dramatic example of wartime scarcities and production. In 1941 the sources of crude rubber from Malaya were lost to the Japanese. By 1943 the Polymer Corporation at Sarnia was producing synthetic rubber, but the new tires ran so hot at first that trucks mounted barrels of water on each side to drip on the tires as the truck rolled along!

Foodstuffs like butter and sugar were also rationed (sugar was restricted to one-half pound per person per week). Alcohol was limited to one 12-ounce "mickey" per month. Prices were also controlled to prevent runaway inflation. Coffee, for example, stayed at about 40 cents a pound; apple sauce in 16-ounce tins sold 2 for 15 cents; maple syrup was 29 cents for a 16-ounce jug. Clothing was rationed, but real silk stockings cost only 69 cents a pair. (It was during the war that nylon stockings first came on the market in a limited way; they were highly praised for their durability and for their trading value in Britain or Europe, for those fortunate enough to have them.) Even real estate came within government regulations. Midway through the war, there was a determined movement to use Roselawn west of Avenue Road for the building of wartime housing. This housing comprised standardized small-frame bungalows that were intended to be torn down after the war. There was much local opposition to this plan, and it was defeated largely through the steady opposition of John Innes. Instead of on Roselawn, the wartime houses were built on Glencairn west of Bathurst Street. Most of them still remain. They were not pulled down after the war, but they have been built upon and converted into forms far different from their original state. Housing prices in North Toronto remained quite close to prewar levels; a solid-brick three-bedroom house in North

DEPARTMENT OF NATIONAL WAR SERVICES
NATIONAL SALVAGE DIVISION

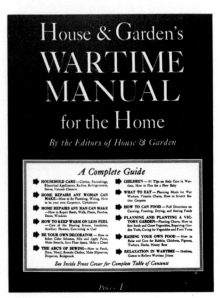

Toronto, complete with fireplace, oak floors and a private drive, was priced at $3,400.

North Toronto produced war heroes, hundreds of them. Anyone who, for $1.30 a day, will submit to the most autocratic leadership for an unspecified period of time surely qualifies as a hero. Once enlisted, one did exactly as one was told, whether that was patrolling the barbed wire of a prison camp in the wilds of Northern Ontario, sleeping under a truck during Italy's torrential spring rains, or riding a tank at midnight through choking clouds of dust at Falaise, expecting a deadly German 88mm anti-tank gun to open up your tank like a sardine can at any moment.

In North Toronto today there are still hundreds of individuals with memories of World War II. Ben Dunkelman, as a junior officer, won the Distinguished Service Cross for bravery in the Canadian drive through the Low Countries and a few years later found himself actually fighting *against* British troops as the officer in charge of the Israeli 7th Brigade in the 1948 war for Palestine. Major Brian S. McCool of Belsize Drive, Beachmaster at the ill-fated Dieppe attack, was wounded, captured, and while in prison camp wrote out from memory much of the lyrics and scores of Gilbert and Sullivan operettas to keep up camp spirits.

The war did one thing very effectively. It ended the Depression. Not only were

In 1941 a squadron of tanks from the Governor General's Horse Guards — "the GeeGee Aitch Gees" — visited Eglinton Park to promote the sale of war bonds. The tanks were brought down from Camp Borden on tank-carriers.

there jobs and money, but there was a sense of energy, a common drive. Canada became a proud nation, taking an important role among the Allies.

For those returning, the north end had changed very little during the war; it was still what today we would call overly respectable and straight-laced. When Ernest Hemingway wrote for the *Toronto Star*, he sneeringly wrote that "85% of the inmates attend a Protestant church on Sunday." This was not far from the truth in the North Toronto of 1945. People were particularly sensitive on issues of liquor and sex. On April 30, 1945, an Air Force officer was ordered out of the Union Station because he kissed his wife in that public place! While this was an isolated incident, it showed that Victorian attitudes were still not uncommon. Pregnant women, for example, were almost never seen in public in 1945.

The returning armed forces had learned a different lifestyle. The north-end soldier who had been ordered to stand guard at a military brothel in Europe would have a hard time explaining that to his mother. (Was it better to kill an enemy than to guard a brothel?) For many, both at home and at war, the war years were their first introduction to alcohol. The friendly pubs of England just never seemed to run out of beer. North Toronto, of course, was dry, and the homey atmosphere of British pubs was hardly reflected in the wartime Jolly Miller at York Mills or the Rosedale Hotel down at Shaftesbury and Yonge. One recalls with amazement the semi-obscure doors saying "Ladies and Escorts"; women, alone or in groups, were not allowed in without a male escort, and it would be a brave man indeed who would take his bride-to-be into a Toronto beverage room. It would be 1947 before the first Toronto "cocktail lounge" was opened downtown, and much later before they reached North Toronto.

What had to happen was a general adjustment. Young returning vets deferred where reasonable to the customs of their elders. The older generations, perforce, began to discard some of their more restrictive rules. Some even began to play golf on Sundays, and some more "advanced" elders drove to Niagara Falls each weekend *to play bridge on Sunday*.

It was a new beginning for each returning veteran. The Department of Veteran's Affairs (DVA) gave each returnee a choice of three settlements: a straight cash gratuity of some $3,500; a university education of equal value; or some $6,000 with which to buy a suburban or rural lot and build on it ($2,500 of this settlement was repayable at $19 a month). Several areas of Willowdale and Newtonbrook were built up in this way, and many of the new small-holders were from North Toronto homes.

Surprisingly enough, there appeared to be jobs for all, in spite of the imminent closing of so many wartime industries. It was reported, for example, that there were 47,000 job openings in the Ontario trucking industry alone. Suddenly money seemed plentiful. Veterans had their gratuities; some who had been prisoners-of-war had the full pay that had built up during their captivity, and sometimes promotions had been automatic, too. Many wives or fiancées had worked through the war while living with their parents and had built up savings and war bonds. Now men and women could make dreams of cohabitation, in its full sense, come true. That dream bungalow, seen so often in magazines and movies, was now possible.

The outbreak of war in 1939 had started an economic revolution as war needs drove up productivity and as competition for workers made for higher wages and prosperity. When the war ended, the energy and drive continued, now directed into personal and local community activities. "A revolution," in the opinion of José Ortegay Gasset, "only lasts 15 years, a period which coincides with the effectiveness of a generation." Civilian leadership during the war years and immediately thereafter was generally very effective; the people of North Toronto produced and supported strong local politicians. In Eglinton riding during the provincial election of 1945, for example, a record percentage of the electorate voted (76%) and gave a plurality of 28,000 to Leslie E. Blackwell.

In 1944 the north end Ward 9 elected two excellent aldermen to represent them, John Innes and Donald Fleming. These two men were prominent among those who established the Planning Board for the Greater Toronto area. It was a forward step in overriding petty local politics and provided a basis on which Metropolitan Toronto could be established in 1953.

One of the most urgent needs for North Toronto was better roads for the rapidly increasing number of automobiles. Yonge Street was crowded, and it ran only north and south, while thousands of homes were being built east and west. The first broadening move for North Toronto, and for burgeoning Leaside, was the building of the Leaside Bridge over the Don Valley to link up with the Danforth area. Previously, the shortest connection in that direction had been a narrow, winding continuation of Bayview Avenue into the Don Valley — the old paved road can still be traced going down the hill — and then up steep Pottery Road to Broadview Avenue. Now there was a more direct connection for North Torontonians who worked in the east end, especially useful as a shortcut to Danforth and the Kingston Road leading to Montreal and points east. There was a plan to run an arterial road from Merton and Mt. Pleasant down the old Belt Line route into the Don Valley and downtown, but this was rejected in favour of what was called the Clifton Road Project. This was the extension of Mt. Pleasant from where it ended at St. Clair down through Rosedale to a connection with Jarvis Street. (One block south of St. Clair on the west side of Mt. Pleasant Road is a very small parkette marking where Clifton Road was cut off to permit Mt. Pleasant to continue south; thus the project was called the Clifton Road Project.) Before this, there had been heavy traffic through Moore Park and down the steep Maclennan Avenue hill into Rosedale.

Eglinton Avenue was finally reopened across the Don. This opened a huge area that became known as the "Golden Mile" in Scarborough, where a huge new Frigidaire plant would soon begin to fill a crying household need. Bayview Avenue was widened, levelled out just south of Blythwood, and then finally extended into the Don Valley and downtown.

In 1946 the huge Sunnybrook Veteran's Hospital was officially opened on Bayview Avenue just opposite Blythwood Road. It was the largest hospital in Canada at the time — and perhaps still is. (To remind us of the cruelties of war, some veterans of the First World War were moved into Sunnybrook Hospital in 1946, having at that time spent nearly 30 years of misery from mustard-gas poisoning.)

In 1946 the Locke Library at Lawrence and Yonge was approved, and it opened in

ELECTRICAL CONSUMPTION

The increasing popularity of electrical appliances in Ontario can be gathered from the following figures showing electrical consumption increasing eightfold while costs dropped by almost half:

	KILOWATT HOURS SOLD	COST PER KW HOUR
1920	215 million	2.01 cents
1950	1,951 million	1.025 cent

1949. At the same time the big, new swimming pool at Eglinton Park was built. Small local improvements were common: for example, the 100-watt streetlights that lit side streets at 100-feet intervals were changed to 300-watt bulbs. Local organizations began to reassemble. In 1945 the YMCA, which had lapsed in 1925 from its home in the old Grundy home at 2 Albertus Avenue, began operations again at the northeast corner of Broadway and Yonge. By 1950 the YMCA had a new building of its own at 130 Eglinton East. There was also a brief revival of local interest in track and field. Eglinton Park saw competitions between such teams as the St. Clements Sharks, the Glengowan Gorillas, the Dawlish Ducks, and the Soudan Squirrels.

Not all the money went into community projects. The number of automobiles doubled in the five years after the war; even then (1950) more than one-half of the homes in North Toronto would still be without a car. Mills and Hadwin, not content to sell cars as fast as they could get them from Windsor, also advertised radios, refrigerators, stoves and washing machines.

As of 1950 Ontario used 25-cycle electric current that produced a disturbing flicker in light bulbs. Most of the rest of North America was on flicker-free 60-cycle current. By 1952 it was decided that the province should be converted to 60 cycle. Starting in 1952 North Toronto was invaded by teams who converted every electric unit — washers, phonographs, even clocks — to the new frequency. It was one of the largest of postwar projects; estimated to cost $2 million, it soon exceeded that and was still going on in 1955.

Homes were being built around the edges of North Toronto. Gradually, over the next few years, farms, golf clubs and airfields would be engulfed by the new suburbs. Nearly all these homes were built one or two at a time, at least in the first few postwar years, by what we would today consider small-time entrepreneurs. For the most part they built one-storey or storey-and-a-half brick houses, but now a garage was usually included. Surprisingly few new construction methods were introduced. In 1947 Walter Page, who had earlier built in Lawrence Park, built two houses on Glenavy Road off Broadway Avenue. The first foundation was dug in the traditional method by a team of horses pulling a scoop-shovel, but for the second foundation he was able to obtain the services of a bulldozer, a wartime development that was to revolutionize earth-moving.

Prosperity was the keynote of the postwar years. This prosperity reached virtually everyone, not just the well-to-do or the comfortably employed. Until the 1940s many

Just to the right of the billboard in the centre of this picture, the railway bridge that still spans Yonge at Merton can be seen. This scene of muddy desolation is now the TTC subway marshalling yards. A storm sewer is being laid down the old valley in the late 1940s. Few pictures reminds us better of the tremendous amount of work involved in piping and wiring laid underground in a modern community. At the corner of Yonge and Eglinton, for example, 24 manholes are needed to access underground.

Looking south at Davisville in 1953 as the Yonge Street subway nears completion. In a few years, apartments would replace the industries in the background, and the head office of the Toronto Transit Commission would arise in the foreground.

people, probably half of all Canadian workers, could have been described as "working poor," those whose work was sporadic, or seasonal, or just poorly paid. Most industries regularly laid off workers for a part of the year. Often these layoffs took place just before Christmas, leaving thousands close to real poverty for the winter, and with little hope of anything but an impoverished old age. The author recalls the sinking feeling in December 1939 as the foreman came down the factory floor with the list of those who were to be laid off. But, re-hired in April 1940, the same employees found themselves virtually locked into year-round jobs. A list of "essential war workers" issued for the Toronto military district was intended to prevent essential workers from joining the armed forces and made almost any change of work difficult.

This kind of security, together with higher wages and the introduction of realistic old-age pensions, changed life for many, if not most, North Torontonians. Now, for the first time ever, a single industrial wage could support a family. From this fact came miles of suburban streets and a booming economy that couldn't produce enough appliances, cars and household furnishings.

By 1954 North Torontonians had access to unemployment insurance, workmen's compensation, family allowances, old-age pensions, and welfare. The turn-of-the-century townsfolk of North Toronto would have had difficulty even imagining such a network of protection from ill-fortune and poverty.

Nor could these townspeople have imagined the medical advances that in the next 50 years would almost double the average person's life span. Killing diseases such as tuberculosis, diabetes and pneumonia came under control through informed treatment and the discovery of new drugs. Dr. George C. Brink, who lived on Blythwood Road, was appointed Director of the Division of Tuberculosis for the Ontario Department of Health in 1935. Under his direction, the provincial death rate from tuberculosis dropped from the highest in Canada to the lowest. Insulin (1922), penicillin (1941), and the Salk vaccine (1954) meant a longer life for hundreds of North Torontonians.

From 1954 onwards, perhaps, the main emphasis seems to have been not on security, but on increasing wealth. In the 1950s incomes would rise (75%) almost three times as fast as the cost of living (28%). In those and later years most North Torontonians, like millions of other North Americans, would find themselves able to live in a style that a Roman emperor would have envied.

From primeval forest, to Indian encampment, to military road, to pioneer farms, to small villages, to fast-growing town, to prosperous suburb — North Toronto in 1954, together with the larger Toronto community, was on the brink of three decades of rapid development that would turn Toronto into the major metropolitan city of today. But even in this era of rapid development, North Toronto retains a distinct sense of community and identity based on the unique history, traditions and artifacts of its past. •

On March 3, 1954, the subway was operating as far north as Eglinton, but the official ceremonies were held at Davisville and Yonge. Premier Leslie Frost is speaking, and Mayor Allen W. Lamport risks the March chill without a hat.

BIBLIOGRAPHY

Adamson, Anthony. "Why not an Aristocracy?" *1837 Remembered*. Toronto: Ontario Historical Society, 1988.

Andre, John. *Infant Toronto as Simcoe's Folly*. Toronto: Centennial Press, 1971.

Armstrong, Frederick H. *City in the Making*. Toronto: University of Toronto Press, 1958.

Arthur, Eric. *Toronto: No Mean City*. Toronto: University of Toronto Press, 1961.

Ashworth, E.M. *Toronto Hydro Recollections*. Toronto: University of Toronto Press, 1955.

Baines, Nancy, et al. *A Student History of North Toronto Collegiate*. Toronto: Casson House, 1987.

Baldwin, R.M. & J. *The Baldwins and the Great Experiment*. Don Mills: Longmans, 1969.

Benn, Carl. *The Battle of York*. Belleville: Mika Publishing, 1984.

Berchem, F.R. *The Yonge Street Story*. Toronto: McGraw-Hill-Ryerson, 1977.

Boylen, J.C. *York Township, an Historical Survey, 1850-1954*. Township of York, 1954.

Bruce, Hon. Herbert A. *Varied Operations*. Toronto: Longmans, 1958.

Bull, Stewart. *The Queen's York Rangers*. Erin: The Boston Mills Press, 1984.

Burnet, Jean R. *Ethnic Groups in Upper Canada*. Toronto: Ontario Historical Society, 1972.

Careless, J.M.S. *Colonists and Canadiens, 1760-1867*. Toronto: Macmillan, 1971.

————. *Toronto to 1918*. Toronto: James Lorimer & Co., 1984.

Careless, J.M.S., and Brown, R. Craig. *The Canadians 1867-1967*. Toronto: Macmillan, 1980.

Chadwick, E.M. *Ontarian Families*. Belleville: Mika Press, 1972.

Charlesworth, Hector. *Candid Chronicles*. Toronto: Macmillan, 1925.

Clark, David E. *Singing the Lord's Song*. Toronto: Eglinton United Church, 1980.

Commemorative Biographical Record of the County of York. Toronto: J.H. Beers and Co., 1907.

Due, John F. *The Intercity Electric Railway Industry in Canada*. Toronto: University of Toronto Press. 1966.

Dunham, Aileen. *Political Unrest in Upper Canada, 1815-36*. Toronto: McClelland and Stewart, 1963.

Dunkelman, Ben. *Dual Allegiance*. Toronto: Macmillan of Canada, 1976.

Elford, J.T. *Canada's Last Frontier*. Sarnia: Lambton County Historical Society, 1982.

Filey, Michael. *A Toronto Album*. Toronto: University of Toronto Press, 1970.

Filey, Michael, et al. *Passengers Must Not Ride on the Fenders*. Toronto: Green Tree Publishing Co., 1974.

Firth, Edith. *The Town of York, 1793-1815*. Toronto: The Champlain Society, 1962.

————. *The Town of York, 1815-1834*. Toronto: The Champlain Society, 1966.

Forman, Debra. *Legislators & Legislatures of Ontario*. Toronto: Ontario Legislature Library, 1984.

Gates, Lillian F. *After the Rebellion*. Toronto: Dundurn Press, 1988.

Glazebrook, G.P.DeT. *Life in Ontario*. Toronto: University of Toronto Press, 1975.

The Golden Years of Trucking. Rexdale, Ontario: Ontario Trucking Association, 1977.

Guillet, Edwin C. *Pioneer Settlement in Upper Canada*. Toronto: University of Toronto Press, 1933.

————. *Life and Times of the Patriots*. Toronto: University of Toronto Press, 1968.

————. *The Pioneer Farmer and Backwoodsman*. Toronto: University of Toronto Press, 1970.

Hallowell, Gerald A. *Prohibition in Ontario*. Toronto: Ontario Historical Society, 1972.

Hart, Patricia. *Pioneering in North York*. Toronto: General Publishing Co., 1968.

Hathaway, E.J. *Jesse Ketchum and His Times*. Toronto: McClelland and Stewart, 1929.

Hounsom, Eric W. *Toronto in 1810*. Toronto: Ryerson Press, 1970.

Illustrated Historical Atlas of the County of York. Belleville: Mika Press, 1972.

Jackes, Lyman. *Tales of North Toronto*. 2 vols. Toronto: North Toronto Business Men's Association, 1948.

Jameson, Anne. *Winter Studies and Summer Rambles....*
   Toronto: Nelson, 1944.
Keilty, Greg. *1837 Revolution in the Canada.*
   Toronto: NC Press, 1974.
Kilbourn, William. *The Firebrand.*
   Toronto: Irwin Press, 1956.
Kyte, E.C. *Old Toronto.*
   Toronto: Macmillan, 1954.
Jones, Robert L. *History of Agriculture in Ontario 1613-1880.*
   Toronto: University of Toronto Press, 1977.
Lemon, James. *Toronto Since 1918.*
   Toronto: James Lorimer & Co., 1985.
Martyn, L.B. *The Face of Early Toronto.*
   Sutton West: Paget Press, 1982.
McBirney, Margaret, and Bigen, Mary. *Tavern in the Town.*
   Toronto: University of Toronto Press, 1987.
McNaught, K.W.K. *The Pelican History of Canada.*
   Markham: Penguin Books, 1969.
Minhinnick, Jeanne. *At Home in Upper Canada.*
   Toronto: Clarke Irwin, 1983.
Mitchell, John. *The Settlement of York County.*
   Toronto: County of York, 1952.
Mulvany, Charles P. *History of Toronto and County of York.*
   Toronto: C. Blackett Robinson, 1885.
Myers, Jan. *The Great Canadian Road.*
   Toronto: Red Rock Publishing, 1977.
Newlands, David L. *Early Canadian Potters.*
   Toronto: McGraw-Hill-Ryerson, 1979.
North Toronto in Pictures 1889-1918.
   Toronto Public Library Board, 1974.
Phillips, Chas. E. *The Development of Public Education in Canada.* Toronto: Gage, 1957.
Rempel, J.I. *The Town of Leaside.*
   Toronto: East York Historical Society, 1982.
Robertson, J. Ross. *Landmarks of Toronto, Vols. I-III.*
   Toronto: s.n., 1894.
———. *The Diary of Mrs. John Graves Simcoe.*
   Toronto: Ontario Publishing Co., 1934.
Correspondence of Hon. Peter Russell, Vols. I-III. Ed. E.A.
   Cruikshank. Toronto: Ontario Historical Society, 1932.
St. John, Judith. *Firm Foundation.*
   Toronto: Metropolitan United Church, 1958.

Scadding, Henry. *Toronto of Old.* Abridged 1966.
   Toronto: Oxford University Press, 1966.
Smith, Nancy Larratt. *Young Mr. Smith in Upper Canada.*
   Toronto: University of Toronto Press, 1980.
Thompson, Austin Seton. *Spadina: the Story of Old Toronto.*
   Toronto: Pagurian Press, 1975.
West, Bruce. *Toronto.* Toronto: Doubleday, 1967.
Wheels of Progress.
   Toronto: Toronto Transportation Commission, c.1940.

Periodicals
Canadian Agriculturalist, passim, 1843-55.
Canadian Monthly, passim, 1879.
Mayfair, March, 1930.
The Observer, passim.
Ontario History, Vol. 54. "The Trials of John Montgomery."
———, Vol. 64. "William McDougall...."
———, Vol. 72. "Sir Francis Bond Head."
Rose Belford's Canadian Monthly, passim, 1878-9.
York Pioneer, 1961, "Oaths of Allegiance before
   William Willcocks, 1800-1806."

Miscellaneous
Garvin, Lucy. Notes from a seminar held at Gibson House,
   Willowdale, by the Periodical Department, Ontario
   Museum Association, 1986.
Home District, *Municipal Council Minutes,* 1842-47.
John Howard's Diaries (abridged) Toronto Historical Board, n.p.
James Lesslie Diaries, 1866-78, Dundas Museum, n.p.
North Toronto Council, *Minutes, 1890-91.*
Ontario Bureau of Archives, *Reports 3,9,10 and 12.*
   Toronto, 1905-14.
Ontario Department of Public Records and Archives.
   Reports 17,18 and 20. Toronto, 1928-32.
Phillip De Grassi Autobiography,
   Todmorden Mills Museum Archives, n.p.
Toronto, *City Council Minutes, 1912.*
Wallace Judd, *Reminiscence of North Toronto,* A talk.
William Tyrell Papers, Fisher Rare Book Library, Toronto.
York Township, *Minutes, 1860-71.*
York, Upper Canada, *Minutes of Meetings and Lists of
   Inhabitants, 1797-1823.*

Street Index

Photo Credits